# Time's Language II

## Selected Poems

## (2019-2023)

*Margaret's Hands*

by Barbara Byers, 2023.

# Time's Language II

## Selected Poems

## (2019-2023)

### Margaret Randall

Introduction by
Katherine M. Hedeen and Víctor Rodríguez Núñez

San Antonio, Texas

2023

*Time's Language II: Selected Poems (2019-2023)*
© 2023 by Margaret Randall

Cover photograph: "Wadi Rum" by Margaret Randall. Poems and cover image from *Stormclouds Like Unkept Promises* used by permission of the author and Casa Urraca Press (Abiquiu, New Mexico: 2022); poems and cover image from *Vertigo of Risk* used by permission of the author and Casa Urraca Press (Abiquiu, New Mexico: 2023); poems and cover image from *Home* used by permission of the author and Casa Urraca Press (Abiquiu, New Mexico: 2023); poems and cover image from *Your Answer is Your Map* used by permission of the author and Bob & Susan Arnold's Longhouse (Green River, Vermont: 2023).

First Edition
Paperback ISBN: 978-1-60940-625-7
E-books ISBN: 978-1-60940-626-4

Wings Press

Wings Press books are distributed to the trade by
Independent Publishers Group
www.ipgbook.com

# Contents

## From *Against Atrocity*
San Antonio, Texas: Wings Press 2019

## From *Starfish on a Beach: The Pandemic Poems*
San Antonio, Texas: Wings Press 2020

## From *Out of Violence into Poetry*

San Antonio, Texas: Wings Press 2020

## From *Stormclouds Like Unkept Promises*

Abiquiu, New Mexico: Casa Urraca Press 2022

## From *Vertigo of Risk*

Abiquiu, New Mexico: Casa Urraca Press 2023

## From *Home*
Abiquiu, New Mexico: Casa Urraca Press 2023

## From *Your Answer is Your Map*
Green River, Vermont:
Bob & Susan Arnold's Longhouse, 2023

## Uncollected Poems

*For my family, born and chosen.*

# Author's Note

In 2018 Wings Press in San Antonio, Texas, released my first selection of poetry culled from 28 books published over the years. *Time's Language: Selected Poems (1950-2018)* had an introduction by Katherine M. Hedeen and Víctor Rodríguez Núñez; they also made the selection. Bryce Milligan curated the beautiful hardcover edition, which also included a selection of photographs and an annotated chronology. *Time's Language II: Selected Poems (2019-2023)* is a continuation of that volume, extending the best of my poetry to the present. This time I made the selection, and the introduction is once again by Hedeen and Rodríguez Núñez, specially written for this new volume. One poem, "Made Rich by Art and Revolution," appears in both books, a bridge carrying readers from one to the other. Once again, Bryce Milligan designed and edited this book, as he has all twenty-one of my books and chapbooks published by Wings Press; I am so grateful for his thoughtful curation and his friendship over the years.

—M.R.

## Made Rich by Art and Revolution

When I am gone, and August comes
to my desert,
rain will soak sand,
its rich scent rising
to enter the lungs of another mother or walker,
someone whose intention and desire
I cannot know.

When I am gone this painting of little islands
miniature trees and birds
floating in a magical sea of blue
will hang in someone else's house.
Will that person tell the story
of poor Nicaraguan peasants
made rich by art and revolution?

A granddaughter may inherit
my turquoise earrings.
The clay pans I've used for years,
their pungency filling the house,
will offer up a new generation
of bread.
Someone not yet born may read this poem.

But who will ask the questions
born of the answers
I juggle today.
Who will know the heat
of this great love,
or catch fragments of my memory
reassembling just before dawn.

# Introduction:

# The poem happens on its own terms

Since the beginning of time, poetry has helped people to confront adversity. This is its reason for being, its public and private utility, its external and internal beauty. This is why it has traversed all the ages, why it accompanies us today, why it will exist as long as we breathe. Verse opposes the adverse, be it natural or artificial, be it social or personal, whatever it be. The poetry of Margaret Randall that summons us here, this powerful *Time's Language II*, confirms it.

✼

*But who will ask the questions*
*born of the answers*
*I juggle today.*

It is fitting that the poem bridging *Time's Language* and *Time's Language II*, the two volumes of Randall's selected poetry, is "Made Rich by Art and Revolution." The title winks at readers, suggesting one of Randall's power political poems, the ones she is best known for, the ones that chronicle a life of deep commitment to social justice. Yet it begins, "When I am gone...." Then, a declaration of vulnerability at the end of the first stanza, "I cannot know." Later, "who will...?" Nostalgia, doubt, conjecture. We are before a subtle shift.

Poetry is questioning, refusing to accept things as they are, rebelling against everything that oppresses us, represses us. Poetry draws strength from its weakness, it is critical even when it is celebratory. Poetry is what's inside a question, the force that drives us to know, and Randall knows this better than anyone.

✳ ✳

*Time opens and closes about itself,*
*marking past, present, and future*
*on all outdated maps.*

If *Time's Language* was in many ways a testament to life already lived, *Time's Language II* is a chronicling of the everyday right now. A witness then to these times, our times. Living with the present, in all its complexity, which also means reflecting on the past. Here there are ghosts, many ghosts. And remembering. And forgetting. And time, lost and found.

Like all true poetry, Randall's defamiliarizes the world, presents it to us as if we were seeing it for the first time. That is to say, poetry offers us vision without the spiderweb of ideologies, which naturalize everything and, above all, what is artificial. The cartographies we use to know where we are, are no longer useful and we need to reinvent them. This has never been the reason for the cartographer but rather the magic of the poet.

＊ ＊ ＊

*The horrors…do not belong*
*in a poem and can only be told*
*in a poem…*

For Randall, poetry is the sacred space, the place for recovery and for redemption. Our right now recounted: the horrors of injustice, of violence and war, and of a pandemic.

Poetry puts us in our place, reaffirms us as human beings and, consequently, as part of the universe. The dominant ideology has made us believe we are superior, we have the right to appropriate things and decide on their fate. Hand in hand with Randall, we enter poetry as a refuge not only against the adversity of the virus, as metonymy of our time, but also against immodesty, greed, solipsism.

＊ ＊ ＊ ＊

*At 84 none of this matters.*
*Earth is on course*
*to shed us like dry skin,*
*and you who are 10 or 24 or 47*
*must take care to preserve*
*those memories we've forgotten.*

Poetry to rescue memory. Randall's right now is ours, but it is also hers alone. A persistent recording of time insists on confronting the intricacies of being old. A rare perspective and a gift to readers. And a lesson, too.

One of the greatest adversities that poetry conjures is forgetfulness. As in *One Hundred Years of Solitude*, it is a remedy against "the plague of oblivion." Oblivion, in social terms, is a lethal weapon, a crime that goes unpunished. Randall's poetry, now and always, is memory and consciousness of memory.

✵ ✵ ✵ ✵ ✵

>*…its name was Voice and it grew*
>*to meet every challenge*
>*fill every space*
>*build a bit of victory in your mouth.*
>*…*
>*I want to say it all before my journey*
>*fizzles and breathes its last.*

A voice of urgency. *Time's Language II* is this, as well. To honor the poetry, to let it happen on its own terms, to give words their due space before time is up.

Randall is a poet who, to a great extent, fulfills a pending task for the poetry of our times: the poetic I overflowing to include others. Poetry must stop being a monologue, become a dialogue, include the reader to the point of becoming a co-author. We must not renounce personal experience, but do as Randall does, understand it as a social experience as well.

✻ ✻ ✻ ✻ ✻ ✻

*We have before us the opportunity–full of privilege and responsibility–to write the true history of our times.*

—from Randall's how-to guide on
testimonial literature, *Testimonios* (1983)

*Time's Language II* takes this opportunity to heart. What is the true history of our times? There is no such thing as impartial. There is no such thing as just one telling. Margaret Randall's poetry offers us a counternarrative to official history in verse, a recognition of the multidimensional reality we live. It is a deeper understanding of our everyday, of how it is personal and political and true.

Since the publication of *Times's Language*, in 2018, Margaret Randall has written and published six books of poems and one plaquette, each represented in this anthology. The book ends with a series of uncollected poems, glimpses of the next. She is an example of the poet's commitment to work: being attentive and surrendering to contemplation, which ultimately results in an intervention in reality. We are ever grateful to Margaret Randall for her illuminating transformation of the adverse into verse.

Katherine M. Hedeen
Víctor Rodríguez Núñez
Mount Vernon, OH
January 31, 2023

From *Against Atrocity*

San Antonio, Texas: Wings Press 2019

## Counting Backward

Counting backward, common practice
at my age, I may stumble upon
the ancient turquoise bead I stooped to gather
from Chaco's purple sand.
I knew I was acting against legality
and moral rightness
when I refused to return that bead
to its millennial seasons.

Continuing to count, I might remember
a conversation pierced by shadow,
that woman who passed us on the trail,
helped when I fell against a rock,
then disappeared when we tried
to thank her: ghosts when least expected,
melodies singing in my head for years,
giving me comfort when alone.

I return to the high temperature
of steadying hands on mine
when the sound of soldier's boots
thunders through my head.
Any soldiers. Any boots. Any war.
I clutch to my breast
the birth of each child,
holding fast its place in body memory.

Counting, I always find your kiss
of prolonged intensity,
lips that thirty years on haven't ceased
to caress mine with their gentle fire.
No need to go backward
to embrace that kiss.
It is with me as I write,
bathes me in permanence.

# Crisscrossing this Generous Nest

The American bison yesterday, like caribou
or wildebeest today, Canada geese,
Monarch butterflies, and salmon
fighting their way upstream:
all follow seasonal instinct, their need
to leave and return etched in the cycle
each journey describes.

Whales swim vast miles to feed, mate
and give birth, their yearly travels
taking them along unraveling coasts
welcoming new generations
as they circumnavigate naval sonar
and other impediments
with determination that astounds.

Magnetic perception, lunar orientation,
landmarks, echolocation, scent
or solar heat:
patterns of movement handed down
from generation to generation
attract and repel whole communities
crisscrossing this generous nest.

We humans too follow patterns laid down
by need. Outcast Europeans
defying oceans to begin again in a new place,
southern Blacks moving north in search
of work and dignity.
Exploration or displacement
depending upon who tells the story.

But male need too often follows a scent
of blood: disappearance, exile, war.
The Middle Passage remembers
foul vessels stuffed with human cargo.
Today's migrations leave a trail
of deflated life vests, abandoned toys,
stories severed before The End.

Man, and it's almost always man, hungers
for war, his obsession requiring
prized properties and obscene advantage
on destruction's giant Monopoly board.
His victims have no choice but to die
while animals—our better selves—follow
the scent of sweet grass, weather, memory.

## The Rains Themselves Make No Excuse

Memory's deft porosity leaves tectonic tremors
on a landscape gone to seed—
every swollen arm of green
withered before the rains.

The rains themselves make no excuse, easier
to thunder through a knot of canyon
than mark time in darkening clouds
above a shifting horizon.

Repeated enough, the replacement story
clings to minds and hearts, erases
the sole of that boot imprinted on lunar dust
or how I love my daughter.

We live in a time of digital double-down
while remembering
—if we are old enough—
the pen's determined journey across paper.

## Every Outdated Map

I curl up at the corner of my living room couch,
look out the window, then quickly
look away. It is 1780, and Cuzco's Plaza
is grim with rain. Micaela wails
as Tupac's body is pulled apart
by horses sent in four directions.

Conquerors from across the sea
are confident the history books
will tell the story as such stories
have always been told:
by judges standing on the sidelines,
owners of all they survey.

I go for a walk in the neighborhood and find
myself in Paris 1792. Change is in the air,
that slant of August light
and rebel voices fully aware
they are organizing a new relationship
between justice and law.

I slip behind the wheel of the old Toyota
on an ordinary Tuesday afternoon,
head to the market
where I buy the most expensive apples
because they are the ones
that taste like fruit.

It is 2017, milk bottles are thick glass once again
and I am a child. Each morning
the milkman leaves two on our back stoop
just as I momentarily reenter today's life
freed from grandfather's invasive fingers
and grandmother's predatory gaze.

On Monday I am 16, discovering the deep chasm
between desire and propriety,
what society says and what it does.
Middle of the night Wednesday to Thursday
I scrape a tabaco kiss
from the sole of one bare foot.

The elevator is broken again and José Benito
pants as he reaches our apartment,
nine floors up, two mattresses
balanced on his head.
He interrupts Doña Leandra telling me
of his death in Estelí.

Time spreads like a 19th century lady's fan
shielding from sight each mouth
that would shout the secrets if it could.
Time opens and closes about itself,
marking past, present, and future
on all outdated maps.

# Every Fear Receives a Million Hits

We thrill to evidence of ancient ingenuity,
discovery of a prosthetic toe
made of wood and leather
in Egypt 3,000 years ago.

We search for solace in numbers,
Fibonacci or Chaos,
calendars that once marked our days,
Golden Proportion's dogged harmony.

Some hover in systems prescribed
by priests or gurus, easier
to follow a leader
than account for this sordid air we breathe.

It only feels like the worst time
because it is *our* time.
Holocausts and genocides also trapped
our parents in omnivorous teeth.

Headlines scream today's news and every fear
receives a million hits.
Time to acknowledge our failures
and don a cloth that fits.

## The World is Flat

An old friend tries to convince me the world is flat.
It wasn't anything she said—
metaphor making a hissing sound
somewhere between memory
and that hard edge you touch
with fingers cut and bloodied from the wars.
It is the place she inhabits
now that colors have changed places at her table.

This is the missing clue: small clouds reflected
in the glassy water of a *tinaja* or water hole
shaped by rock. Heat rising off that rock,
diminishing the water in that hole,
rendering it shallower and dryer
until there is nothing left but dust
swirling around tiny shrimp-like beings
curled into stasis until the next rains.

This could only happen upon a flat earth, not round
as the scientists would have us believe
but stretching from earliest language
to the long thin note of an Indian flute
on air that moves across the worn ropes
of a bridge sagging and ragged
over yet another body of water whispering softly
to itself. There is always another body of water

somewhere. Caught up in the round planet story—
distant poles and elastic band
at its fattened waist—
we have ignored all evidence
while keeping the terrible secret
to ourselves: a land
that moves off as far as an eye can see,
beyond all pain and reason.

The small puffy clouds remain imprinted in dust
as they once glistened on water's surface.
The flute's single note refuses to die
in our hopeful ears.
We know the rains will come
and the tiny shrimp will resume what's left
of their sixteen-day cycle. We are only who we are
right now, in this instant of clarity.

## Memory Rounds the Corner

Memory rounds the corner, wild hair
streaming behind.
She comes to a sudden stop,
unfamiliar landscape
rising on all sides.
Glaciers retreating from the heat
of lies.
Street signs in a language
she might have heard in childhood
but no longer understands.
A harvest of toys with shattered wheels.
Headless dolls.

She decides to return the way she came
but finds her path
overgrown with weeds,
fragments of words
caught in the branches of trees.
Memory tries to scratch the itch
that blooms across her skin
but there is no relief.
Then a portal of hope
beckons her tired flesh
and she follows a multitude of laughing ghosts
to a place where pain cannot survive.

# The Verb *to break*


There's that admissible breakage
we've learned to call
collateral damage.
You can break your metaphorical back,
a child's will (never a metaphor),
sacred trust, even unjust law.

*Forgive me*, he grovels, *I promise
it won't happen again.*
Applying makeup to broken skin,
his wife rehearses her story,
listens to her husband's plea, avoids
his eyes already filled with future threat.

Years after her father's rage, the artist calls
her painting *Daddy Will Spank*,
refers to the child's arm in its sling
as negative space.
And yes, it was her arm.
And yes, he broke it.

One says *I'm broke* and is down a couple million
in preferred stock.
For another the same words
mean she must choose between rent,
buying food or the epinephrine pen
keeping her child alive.

When mass graves emerge across a map
of relentless war, bones shear
from other bones. Human breakage
reveals the landscape we birth
from what the verb *to break*
tells each of us.

## She Knows

1

She knows about stairs,
how they climb
into dwellings
thinking to stay forever.

She knows about angles
—too steep
or too narrow.

The one missing step
where the big man
placed his weight
upon its gentle shoulder.

The steps where your infant head
still reverberates like a drum
after 54 years.

The corner landing,
the up
that became down.

And those stairs
that do not fit

into houses
but rise resolutely
and wander off
a knowing smile on their lips
until their heads are lost
in billowing cumulus.


2


She knows the body
cleaving in two:
new life that will take itself
beyond her borders
with or without a father's
blessing:
a human being
on its magnificent journey.

Nothing will ever be
so singular
or treacherous.


3


She knows wars born of power's greed,
won only in power's imagination,
lost again and again
on the field.

And she knows that field
is where we live
and die.

4

She knows where she is going
if not always
how to get there.

She knows what she wishes
she did not know
but only she can know
on the prickly skin
of this Socratic underbrush
its hidden surprises
lying in endless wait.

# 2020[1]

In secret, we prepared the hundredth anniversary
of our right to vote,
passed the word from mouth to ear,
surprising those who didn't get the message
—one dead battery in a sub-scalp receptor
or faltering pulse on a wrist
exhausted by being forced to wave
when the dictator's carrot-colored mop
roared past along the Avenue.

A few received the invitation
in the old-fashioned way:
faint murmur on a hidden IPhone-12
deep in a camouflaged pocket
among the folds of her all-weather shift,
arthritic thumbs tapping the text,
calling women from every city
and holding pen,
every factory and field.

---

1   This poem was commissioned for what was going to be a collec-
tion commemorating female voting rights in the United States. Each
participant was asked to pick a year from which to write. I picked
2020, the hundredth anniversary of that victory. The anthology never
materialized. When I wrote this poem, I didn't suspect that just a
few years later a woman's right to choose would be taken from us by
a majority right-wing Supreme Court, and our vote would become
more important than ever.

Three years since choice was permitted
the female masses:
corn rows, fuscia hair, hijab
or androgyny,
along with abortion and other rights.
All punishable now by menacing fines
passed into law on moonless nights
by robotic vote
in the only governmental chamber left.

Some of us didn't fight,
didn't believe it
a priority struggle.
Others feel skinned alive.
Now all we want is to remember.
By the time we ignored the 2018 midterms
the holding pens were full
and fully guarded,
our energy's power fizzling to fear.

In clandestine story-circles taking us back
to consciousness raising groups of old
grandmothers told the young
*you don't appreciate what you have
until it's gone.*
Suffrage seemed ill equipped
against all that money and influence,
fake news and alternate truth
replacing simple talk, life as it used to be.

The commemoration had
its forward agenda,
was held in a place I won't reveal
in case we must use it again.
I'll only say its eco-system
was light as air
and solid as ancient stone.
Each woman's travel
came from her ability to dream.

The dark walls of our secret place
were covered with images:
horned masks
challenging rude authority,
horses and bison from millennia past
running free in a time so deep in memory
we could not imagine
how we lived together
in its freedom.

Today on those walls we inscribed phrases
by Sappho, Coatlique,
Simone de Beauvoir, Rosa Luxemburg
Madam Binh, Malala Yousafsai
and Audre Lorde.
Someone brought an old copy
of *The Handmaid's Tale* from Canada,
and a woman from Topeka asked:
*why read in fable what we live each day?*

Millions exited that place, a long stream
moving as far as the eye could see,
an endless mass
of women empowered by the art
on its walls, the stories we needed to hear.
We issued forth into every street and plaza,
field and country lane,
vowing never again
to let them count us out.

Now we rise in numbers great enough
to undo the damage wrought
by these four years,
reclaim our Lysistrata place
among people bearing witness everywhere:
women
and men who offer us their honest hands,
genders that have yet
to speak their names.

On this commemoration of our
hard-earned right to vote,
joined in symbolic ceremony
with those used and abused
in every nation
on our suffering earth,
we take back what they stole
and hold it safe for those who will claim
the future we bequeath them.

## Memory as a Physics Problem

Tissue thin, as if pressed between the pages of a book
or vivid for some who weren't even there
but merely heard the story's echoes,
memory has become a physics problem.

I caress the images lighting my long night's sky
but other versions claim equal space,
answer the questions as they can,
solve the puzzle shamelessly.

A distant sound of war in newsflash cackle
stains plush upholstery with fear.
My father at the wheel of our secondhand Ford,
December 7, 1941.

Seven decades and we're still in that car, my child's fingers
pressed into its backseat isolation,
parents' mute shoulders shunning my pleas,
connection tumbling like dominoes.

Memory inhabits the man on the bridge or you on the couch,
your courageous fingers reaching to ignite my own,
our promise of life together born in that instant,
distance without a before or after.

The man on the bridge holds 1973 in his hands, you 1986,
my parents, long dead, 1941—or maybe not.
Translating sound and smell, voice and touch,
is the problem now.

If the survivor chooses not to speak of genocide,
a raped woman refuses to name her attacker,
silence alters memory's shape
but cannot erase its content.

Where matter and energy join loss and fire,
memory is never singular.
A current of truth parts a sea of lies,
turning all equations inside out.

From *Starfish on a Beach:*
*The Pandemic Poems*

San Antonio, Texas: Wings Press 2019

*Starfish on a Beach*

THE PANDEMIC POEMS

MARGARET RANDALL

Recipient of the 2019 Haydée Santamaría Medal from
Casa de las Americas, the 2019 Poet of Two Hemispheres Prize,
and the 2020 AWP George Garrett Award

## Statistics

The pundits give us graphs,
projections with
different colored lines
representing China, Italy,
our own United States.

They move from left to right
rising gentle or dramatic
but too often in ascent,
giving us hope or telling us
we are headed for disaster.

Statistics have always been
suspect, coming
as they do from minds
endeavoring to comfort
or alarm.

Context is too often missing,
that terrain where
we may consider
time, space, imagination
or our own collective response

in this race to understand
what we should think
and how we must act
before the lines become
a web that traps us in its weave.

## Beneath the Waves

This is a time when we
summon tears
that don't come,
grief hiding like the current
that pulls a body
beneath the waves.

This is a time when a smile
may not be a smile
even in translation
but a stand-in for where
our eyes would go if they
were open to a future tense.

*Be afraid, very afraid*: is the
mantra of those who
benefit from our despair.
*Breathe, breathe deep*
whisper those
who have been here before.

## State of Exception

It is an epidemic and then
a pandemic,
an outbreak in some reports,
a flareup or surge
when the numbers rise,
a leveling off
when they fall.

In some cities the numbers
double every week,
in others every day
or they may even triple
or quadruple
as more people are tested
and fiction becomes fact.

What we call the virus
is important
for getting us to take
it seriously or keeping us calm.
The message is everything
when advertising is the dogma
by which we live and die.

Perhaps we should pair
these names

with terms like nationalism,
class bias, race war, gender parity
and our unwillingness
to welcome those who come to us
escaping death by other means.

We must not allow
the facemask
to become a blindfold,
social distancing
to become disdain,
or a state of exception
to become our lives.

# Spiral

We are learning a new language,
virtual pronunciation
we practice daily

absent the spoken word
in this era
of discordant isolation.

We have time, all the time
in the world
until we have none.

If the pandemic moves
in spiral,
all the graphs are wrong.

All the statistics beliefs
we hardly remember
as the virus comes to stay.

To learn to think in spiral
means ridding ourselves
of arrogance:

We are no safer than, no better
than, no whiter
or more citizen than.

Divesting ourselves of covert pride
we ride the spiral
to a wiser place.

# Eighty Times More

We now know the first person with
COVID-19 was in Wuhan, China
on December 1, 2019. A place
we didn't think about before.

One hundred twenty days to date, at first
not perceived as exceptional and then
entering our consciousness
with the force of every lie and truth.

Forty thousand have died from the virus
in this time of worldwide crisis.
But they are not the only deaths
we record in these 120 days.

In the same period, close to three million
(80 times more) have died of hunger,
1.2 million (33 times more) because they
had no access to medical care.

Ninety-six thousand (two and a half
times more) women died
from lack of rudimentary attention
giving birth and 672,000 infants

(18.1 times more) were born dead
for the same reason.
Statistics can be suspect but there is
only one way to interpret these.

This is not about subtraction but addition,
not to minimize the Corona deaths
but also consider these others
on which we've turned our backs.

Death from hunger is as slow and painful
as lungs filling with bloody fluid
in a world where none of these atrocities
need happen.

# From *Out of Violence into Poetry*

San Antonio, Texas: Wings Press 2020

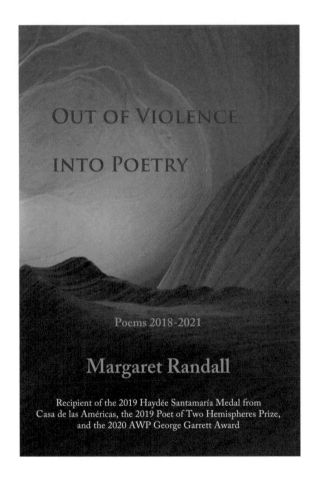

OUT OF VIOLENCE

INTO POETRY

Poems 2018-2021

Margaret Randall

Recipient of the 2019 Haydée Santamaría Medal from
Casa de las Américas, the 2019 Poet of Two Hemispheres Prize,
and the 2020 AWP George Garrett Award

# One Tectonic Plate Slipping Beneath Another

*For Barrett*

It was a continent, robust with mountains
and deserts, alive with a song
that promised forever.

But the land suddenly rifted, one tectonic plate
slipping beneath another, threatening
to take you with it into oblivion

to a place where sound becomes sight
and then again sound,
familiars flee your spirit

leaving you adrift
where nothing
is what it was. Nothing.

Until, floating in that same sea, someone
always there in the wings
swims up beside you,

takes your hand, looks into your eyes
and tells you it's okay
to start again. Yes, she says, late

as it is. Yes, she smiles without need
of words. Yes and yes in this
other life that couldn't have predicted itself.

## Out of Violence into Poetry

Water, real or illusory, shimmers along
the desert horizon.
*Oasis*: early 17th century word
via late Latin from the Greek,
perhaps of Egyptian origin.

Egypt, a country of vast sand
where wet and fertile
exceptions nourish life.
Also: peaceful area or period
in the midst of troubled times.

Thus, place becomes time in the blink
of geography's eye.
Double helix embracing itself
as it rises in our throats:
see-saw of intuition singing loud.

Let me satiate your thirst, feed
your hunger. Satisfy mine,
if only because we are
conscious beings standing together
in this dangerous century.

We are reduced to small gestures:
reflected in a gaze
or touch of a hand,
oases of light where we may move
out of violence into poetry.

## Voice

Voice said what it was born to say
even when high school teacher
father and husband
took pains to contain it.

Pains: exemplary, decorated ones.
You wouldn't know it though.
Impossible to go against
such forces of nature.

Voice snuggled between the sheets
wouldn't eat its vegetables
sounded high-pitched
sometimes landed with a thud.

But its name was Voice and it grew
to meet every challenge
fill every space
build a bit of victory in your mouth.

## Lifetime Warranty

Age wears on the body parts
and I imagine a shop
where replacements are shelved
by model and date,
the experimental or mass-produced
on special sales tables
daring us to try a plastic nose
immune to sun damage
or super batteries for heart or liver
guaranteed to last forever.

Generic models would attract
the low-income shopper,
luxury versions the elite who
*have everything* but a perfect working body.
The dispensary itself might be
an upscale boutique or big box store
where everyone goes for bargains
though no remedies yet for serious cancers,
dementia or flesh-eating bacteria.

Short-term solutions are advertised
in glowing terms and offered
on brightly decorated racks
right beside the cashier:

They just may get you on the way out
and there is no layaway.
This month's special
is portable oxygen in tropical flavors.
No shortage of deception when hope wears thin.

I imagine visiting such a futuristic shop,
boutique or bargain basement,
and know it's a First World dream.
Desperate people everywhere
sell body parts: hair and kidneys,
or use their organs to carry contraband.
If lucky they may get enough to eat
for a few more months,
a fleeting chance at another day.

What would a lifetime warranty mean
to a body wearing only hope?
Will the consumer hold out for designer DNA
or invest in replacement body parts?
How can those who sell a piece of themselves
be sure a sliver of spirit or strand of character
isn't lost in that deal of last resort?
Privilege stalks the rich
while the poor hope only for survival.

# Tongue Seeking Solace

*For Roberto Tejada*, as I ponder his
*Still Nowhere in an Empty Vastness*

A word is uttered. Its echo dances
through time
and cannot be taken back.
Its silhouette expands
across this map
filling every secret corner.

Breath explodes against rock,
early morning dew
beads upon your lip.
You taste salt
as your tongue seeks solace
between your teeth.

This word was meant to follow
in the wake of that.
Feeling remains
the better part of mind.
We grab as much
as we can hold.

Ancestors drag us back
in *cuenta regresiva*

from that stone notch
where the sun's dagger
meets a future
we do not dare to dream.

Can we inhabit simultaneity
of time and place,
imagine
parting the waters
one more time
to reach where we have been?

## Molecules Sometimes Wonder

*"No ideas but in things..."*
—William Carlos Williams


Beneath the seconds I hear a clock ticking
in a language I once knew.
Beneath the minutes, pathways fade
on frayed maps, their faces turned
to a sputtering midnight sun.
The hours are weighted with surplus food,
the sort that comes in UN packaging,
pale blue with white letters:
desperate invitation to survive.

I carry those days and weeks and months
on a back bent by the poundage of hope
in a world still moving only in one direction:
forward, although its molecules
sometimes wonder whether they are
coming or going.
We press time for new possibilities,
intuit a future long gone
or just around the corner.

I may claim our past
will rise again
or all time is simultaneous

rather than sequential.
I can imagine realities as impossible
as the airplane in 1850
or computers back when I longed
for my first Royal portable.
I can play da Vinci to your doubting Thomas.

But that won't provide the extra year
a woman with cancer hopes she has
or the food needed by a child of war
so she may reach adulthood.
Imagined time still meets
the mundane cousin standing in its way
with broad shoulders,
arms akimbo and all the ballast
of a 390-pound running back.

When it comes to assessing matter,
the movement of atoms, quarks,
string theory, loops, the singularity
at the center of a black hole
or where we are going or have been,
there is only our body's story
etched in a mind that is also flesh,
the perfect location
when approached from all directions.

## Each Toy Argues its Future

Training begins emphatic
and early
with nurseries painted pink or blue.

Each toy argues its
future identity:
fighter planes or dolls

so men will learn to attack
and women
receive their blows.

A proper education continues
as children of all genders
are taught to stay

within the lines. Each number
calls forth a color,
each obedience a round of applause.

And what's this about other genders?
They assure us only two
are sanctioned by God and Flag.

Patriots follow the piper's tune,
gamble on
short-term satisfaction.

Meanwhile, those ready to leap
off that safe and rigid map
discover we are the toymakers.

# The Hole October Leaves

I open my eyes and October is gone.
She ducked out while I slept
taking a birthday
and twenty boxes of Girl Scout cookies
a preteen was selling
door to door.

The hole October's left has ragged edges,
a coastline where the struggle for justice
stands on shifting sands
before it succumbs
to fortune tellers
lying through rotten teeth.

There are rules, the big men say,
and they must be followed.
No room for an idea
that sets its own place
at table, does its own dishes,
makes its own bed.

To those who say that's woman's work,
the joke's on you.
Generations fold October's hologram
in sweaty hands,
hold within it the only answer
tough enough to last.

I close my eyes for a second
that feels like centuries:
the loneliness of a hospital ward
where 40 women long to hold
their newborns, Columbus stumbling
upon an inhabited continent,

John Brown's stand at Harper's Ferry,
Trujillo painting the Massacre red,
Ho Chi Minh entering Hanoi,
Che at the Yuro Ravine
and me—still trapped
at Tlatelolco.

October is gone. I look to
all the horizons
thinking I catch sight
of a moving shadow
but only the calendar's empty page
stares back.

# With Memory Clinging to My Back

My memory taps me
on the shoulder,
boasts it is longer
and sharper than I.

It brings up 1959,
the revolution
in Cuba had just
been victorious

and I'd begun to think about
creating justice
in a world where justice
must fight subterfuge.

That year an editor told me
my novel was no good,
suggested I go home,
marry and have some kids:

advice given to women
back then
whether our dream
was doctor or poet.

My memory reminds me
that was the moment
my life appeared to split.
I saw revolution

and art wandering
separate paths
and struggled to
pull them together:

not wife and mother or
poet and revolutionary
but all of the above
because I never doubted

I would do it all, fail
then do it better,
memory always
clinging to my back.

# Those Memories We've Forgotten

*For Cedar Sigo*

At 10 I was terrified when lies rose
among the blades of grass
waving their treacherous arms
and threatening
to suck the breath
from between my teeth.

At 24 the tiny animals that lived
beneath my breastbone
began to wander in different directions.
Some struggled to gain altitude
while others hoped no one noticed them
sheltering in place.

They took the warnings seriously,
wanted to stay
on the right side of history.
But what is the right side of history?
By the time I was 47
camouflage had lost its appeal.

Sun wasn't slanted right for the shadow
I kept pasted to my foot.

We slip in and out
of the stories they tell
in our name,
fear our deepest intuitions.

At 84 none of this matters.
Earth is on course
to shed us like dry skin,
and you who are 10 or 24 or 47
must take care to preserve
those memories we've forgotten.

## Memory and Echo Play Together
## in a Modern-Day Garden of Eden

Memory and Echo play together in
a modern-day Garden of Eden
where only invisible flowers bloom
and someone is designing a fountain
for every season.

Such gardens appear here and there
at the bleakest of times,
ready to welcome those who survive
exploitation, false promises
and patriarchal deception.

Echo brings us the strains of spirituals
sung on ghost ships
crossing the Atlantic
packed with the bodies of slaves
dreaming of their African home.

She carries the cries of natives
forced to leave their lands
and march west, the sighs of women
through centuries of grief,
dependence and subservience.

Memory takes Echo's hand, asks for
this dance and all future dances
along garden paths
that welcome an era in which
every flower grows.

From *Stormclouds Like Unkept Promises*

Abiquiu, New Mexico: Casa Urraca Press 2022

## About the Light

It's about the light so you must spend
sometime in shadow, emerge
with your eyes and every pore
open to receive the brilliance of landscape
without it blinding you.

Cold like heat warms our fingertips
if only by contrast in those places
where embodiment cancels the answer
that didn't come, the wall that should have
had a door in its history of stone.

If you explain everything in relation
to everything else
you miss what disappears between,
becoming dust then rising
like a Phoenix in your hands.

What touches you and what escapes
on ultraviolet beams
or caresses your brow with gentle music
and cool hands is only on loan
for as long as you live.

After that it's no longer your problem
to solve from first gulp of air
to last voice heard:
all that busyness that keeps us
from the work that matters.

## Still Life, Winter 2021

The man wearing resignation and a battered sign
at Carlisle and Constitution
carries a broken history
in the pocket of his Salvation Army coat.
He owns the corner like a drug dealer
but only collects enough
to survive day by day.
He is not into profit, only endurance
which for him means a bed
at the shelter and sustenance enough
to battle weather.

The man doesn't know he's entered this poem
that cannot pretend to tell his story.
The bridge that connects us
has been repossessed by a power
indifferent to us both.
I roll down the window, put a one or a five
in his outstretched hand,
answer *God bless you* with *Stay safe*
and move on, wondering
what questions have been silenced
on our lips.

# Every Death an Act of Survival

*For Sister Dianna Ortiz, 1958-2021*

Sister Dianna Ortiz died today
and yesterday and every day
since that monstrous death
32 years ago. Every death
an act of survival.

The men who stubbed 100 cigarettes
out on her back and raped her
would have said if asked
they were good Christians
fighting Communism.

The horrors she endured do not belong
in a poem and can only be told
in a poem: suspension over an open pit
where dead and living bodies
wiped her memory of all she'd known before.

They forced her to kill and filmed her
as she did: abuse enough to break
an army of angels
justified by their need of a weapon
to keep her in their line of fire.

Foul words describing foul acts
are painful to hear but we
must hear them, absorb them,
understand what is done in the name
of all who would hide such truths.

Word got out: worldwide clamor
for her release and suddenly
an American was there, taking her
away in his car. Afraid he would
kill her, she managed to escape.

Later she thought the mysterious
man might have been there
all along, directing the others.
Later there was abortion.
Later there was madness,

unable to recognize her family
or the sisters in her order,
near failure to function
in this blindered world
that refuses to look or listen.

Years of agony relived, yet
telling her story
each time it was needed,
years that brought fresh deaths
and misplaced shame.

You do not heal from such terror
without necessity's embrace.
You do not heal from it
in each successive death
and certainly not in a poem.

Dianna dies in this poem
and also lives in it:
the Ursuline nun and teacher
whose insistent questions helped bring
Guatemalan fascism to its knees

and force the United States
to admit its role
in a phantom war
denied from one administration
to the next.

Dianna survived her deaths
and lives in this poem
whose reason for being
is to let her go
in peace.

## My Mother's Breasts

Mother crossed the room, body-moisture-scented
from her bath, dark nipples magnets
to my child's eyes. That was before
the word we couldn't speak robbed her
of one, leaving drains and bandages
in its place. Before Dad
failed to hide his repulsion
and Mother's shame devised the story
she would retell for years.

Sister lived with that fear, tried to excise
two healthy glands until she died
of every other ill. I cared for our mother
but never expected the disease in me.
Instead, I thrust my small knobs out
before me under cashmere sweater set,
prayed my golf balls would become
footballs—sports metaphors
framing our stories then.

Yearning for that magical thing
called cleavage,
suffering every breath-defying uplift,
believing exhibition was feeling

until the quiet rhythm
of a baby suckling brought the extasy
of mother/child bond.
Lovers rarely gifted me
that tenderness of touch.

Now, freeing two drooping bags
from all constraint, I live
uninhibited, unencumbered
and alive. My breasts are finally mine
as are my sagging belly and unshaven legs,
mine in all they have endured
and made.
Rewinding a lifetime of punishment
I reignite pleasure on my skin.

# Your Story, Your Escape

*For Ammiel Alcalay*


Start with the right name and you'll find
yourself following the rises and falls
on a map that spreads its arms, carries you
forward even with eyes shut tight.

Open one, then the other, until you can fix
your gaze on the horizon. The temperature
of nixtamal accompanies you, a memory
of pastel dwellings about to repeat themselves.

If you fall into step, there will be clues, moments
of conviction, excision of doubt.
If you don't, there is still no turning back.
The sky is already menacing, the rain torrential.

You are alone on this journey, no one
to comfort or keep you warm,
every sound a milepost where you may stop
and rest, but not for long. No breath will keep you.

Then, in a rush that recalls the furious wings
of migratory birds, you will be joined
by everyone who ever lived and all those
not yet born. This is your story, your escape.

# Medusa

Her hair fanned out from her face:
furious snakes,
writhing in the light of day.

Each strand sent a message
into space but the static
made them hard to decipher.

*Boys will be boys*, the mortals
whined.
But the warning came back

that looking into Medusa's eyes
would turn you to stone.
Why chance it?

Perseus thought her head would
make a powerful weapon
and took it for his arsenal.

The eyes still worked, still paralyzed
those they gazed upon.
*Rape*, cried those eyes, unblinking.

## Talk is Cheap

Heart of Sky, Feathered Serpent and other deities
all worked tirelessly to create humans
capable of keeping the days.

Failing again and again, they resorted
to yellow and white corn,
fashioned beings who spoke.

But talk is cheap, can sound like barking dogs
as some of their descendants
would say.

Keeping the days requires knowledge
of past and future, an ability
to see in every direction.

Go where I go, see what I see, hear
what I hear and then draw
your own map.

There is no pot of gold,
only cadmium red,
all the way down.

## Prometheus Punished

Mob Boss in any era, he laughed at the rest of us.
His crime wasn't hot-wiring cars or selling dope
on a street corner of his choosing
but stealing fire from the gods
and bequeathing it to humanity.
Big deeds, befitting his godfather role.

The gods had to make him an example
and bound him to a rock.
The sentence was eternal torment:
they sent an eagle to peck at his liver
which grew back each day
only to be devoured again the next.

And Prometheus receded into the rock,
became the rock, tried to escape
his sentence by embracing his reputation.
If he was bad, he would be the worst,
serial trickster
in the image of Everyman.

We argued about his crime. Capital offense
or misdemeanor? Aberration or mirror
held to our own behavior?
He bribed us with fire, tried to convince us
he was giving us protection, status,
something only his connections could provide.

The Lord whose mission was to save the world
inadvertently taught us to save ourselves,
convinced us that by saving ourselves
we were also saving the world.
And for centuries few noticed
he'd left half humanity out. Women.

Afterthought or forethought, presented
as Pandora's Box but box in any case:
a container filled with all the secrets and lies,
tricks and vulnerabilities we embody.
To acknowledge us is to free us,
to see us to empower us.

The mobster is one with the rock,
sentenced to agony, life after life.
Boyish charm is a myth of another time.
Ours demands we work for every human
who understands: culture that
moves us forward never kills.

## Drops of Blood on White Snow

Drops of blood on white snow, and
don't forget she was sewing:
the ultimate womanly skill.
Poison apples, mirrors that won't lie
and a glass slipper lost at the dance.

The men either princes or dwarfs,
culmination of desire
or small helpers: safe supporting roles
in these dramas
that fold as neatly as a flag.

The same instructions live in different tales,
waiting to reach out and grab you,
all pointing in the same direction,
meant to make frightened women
of unsuspecting girls.

These metaphors, mixed or not, beckon
like seductive cairns, signals
telling us stop or go
according to each era's
temperature.

The rules change depending on time
and place: more God

equals less freedom,
imagination always follows
lightning home.

It's no accident these bedtime stories
were meant to strangle our lives,
keep us coming back for more.
Sleep well, my daughter,
and don't forget to dream!

## Gretel and Hansel

They leave a trail of crumbs
that are eaten
by hungry animals and birds,
nothing left
for the return.

Then they leave stones,
round and smooth
as if polished by the sea.
These prove
more reliable.

No version of this story
scatters words
in the branches
of trees or folded
into the wind's throat.

And none leaves scraps of fear
rendered invisible
by the magnet of your courage
as you trace
a geography that works.

Gretel and Hansel are lost
in the forest

of their abandonment
but neither gluttony's trap
nor sweet temptation do them in.

Contrary to almost every other
tale—legend or myth—
it is Gretel
who out-smarts
the evil witch.

We are proud of our heroine
when she kills the enemy
and leads her brother home
laden with riches enough
for a happy ending.

A happy ending? Really?
Their father is glad to see
his children again
but their mother is dead.
Someone always has to die.

## Backward Feet

Those Caribbean demons will fool you every time:
Ciguapa of the Dominican Republic
or Trinidad and Tobago's Douen, their backward feet
leading to confusion when you chase them
through dark forests or over burning sand.

That seductive woman you find so attractive
may be a Succabus, the female witch
who will lure you to her lair, have her way
with you while you try to escape
and before you've deciphered those turnabout prints.

These demons are tricky, cover their rotting faces
with wide-brimmed hats,
their cloven hooves beneath the graceful folds
of flowing skirts. Tropical leaves become snares
and only the telltale rattle of chains betrays them.

Beware the Soucouyant, voracious mother
of them all, who sheds her skin
with the setting sun, becoming a ball of fire
that can shrink to slip through any crevice or crack
when pursuing her victim.

What the chroniclers didn't know is that all these
evil beings have OCD. If you sprinkle

grains of rice or salt on the ground before them,
they'll be obliged to stop and count each one,
giving you time to get away.

You cannot turn those deceptive feet around
but you can turn from violence
to kinship, consider desire from an angle
apart from that practice of conquest
you inherit and pass on.

Better yet, don't let yourselves be lured
by the legends, a travel brochure
that promises voluptuous native women
along with your room at a five-star resort
and moonlit evenings in paradise.

Paradise is never paradise when you force
yourself onto the hotel maid who
only wants to live her life and feed her family,
the woman who has learned hope
and hate in equal measure.

# Malintzín

Her mother, poor with many children to feed
sold her to a European who came from afar
seeking to build an empire:
human trafficking just one legacy.

Her new master shared her with friends,
military men all, their armor
an advantage against
the white man's flag.

Malintzín was eight when she was taken.
Wise about meaning, she quickly
learned their language, dreamed in vain
of her brother's school.

Weaving her resistance of words, she bridged
warring cultures, bolstered the invader's
reputation—Stockholm response
to her new master?

But then she was pregnant, gave birth
to a son whose features mirrored hers.
And he too was seen as different,
bullied.

They might have said her skirt was too short
or blouse too tight, accused her of the crime.
Anyone could see her proud stance
as invitation.

Blame the victim has long been patriarchy's
response to women's pain, multiplying
our cruel experience.
But this was the 16<sup>th</sup> century

and Malintzín's reputation preceded her.
In all her glory she was the prisoner:
grave disadvantage
to this day.

They say she slept with the enemy, call her
traitor, mother of impurity,
her life a betrayal, symbol of
all they fear.

Five centuries later not much has changed
for girls and women: the burden
of proof is still on us.
Plan your escape now.

## Waiting Our Turn

Lawrence, he of Lady Chatterley,
said the way to eat a fig
was open it until it becomes
a glittering, rosy, moist, honied,
four-petalled flower,

then after raping the blossom
hold it in your mouth
lick the crack
and devour the flesh
in a single bite.

Every fruit has its secret
said the poet women loved,
who turned us into luscious fruits
to be peeled by hungry lips
then spit out.

Neruda, he of communist
solidarity, wrote
of women's bodies as white hills
and white thighs, promised
to forge us as weapons—

arrow to bow, stone in its sling—
so he could outlive himself.

This poem is my reply.
Neither seductive fruit
to be savored and discarded

nor white in a world of brown
and never ever weaponized,
we sharpen our tongues,
imagine our revenge
and wait our turn.

## Writing the Future

Memory rents a room in my aging flesh
a place to retire on weekends
or for the summer although
when the southern hemisphere summer
recedes in cold rain
and the whales return to Punta del Este
we embrace the northern hemisphere
its dust devils lurching
in drunken desert dance.

The room is small and sparse
with just space enough
for a bed and writing desk
a narrow armoire that can hold
a change of clothes or two
a bathroom down the hall
it must share with other borders
who have set up residence
through my years.

She is the perfect guest
makes few demands
and you won't hear a sound
after ten o'clock at night.
I know she is writing a long poem
of the world, endless verses

that take us from her birth
in a northern New Mexican village
to the summit of Mount Everest and back.

But never back to that village, no,
our journeys go only
in one direction: shooting stars
through the spiral convolutions
of space. We are
always pilgrims on our way
to a new and better world
writing future
with the promises of the past.

# From *Vertigo of Risk*

Abiquiu, New Mexico: Casa Urraca Press 2023

## Dearest Ruth

Dearest Ruth, thank you for coming
if only in my dream.
Your visit surprised me
after the awkwardness between us
last time we spoke.

Of course, I knew you were raging,
confined as they had you,
longing for the Lakewood Avenue house
and your morning walks
around Fresh Pond.

You asked if I'd read your piece on Proust.
I said yes.
You asked what I thought
and I told you it's not finished,
you need to end with a warning, I said,

about consumer capitalism, use Hillary
as an example.
And then wondered
why I ever thought
I should give you advice.

Your addiction to a great man
surely allowed you
to understand the writer
who needed seven books
to explore the psychology of memory.

In my dream you reminded me
our memory was born
in that country where we met,
that country like a broken body now,
struggling to breathe.

Loving you as I did, I'm glad
you didn't live
to see it all come undone,
the questions we nurtured
disappearing on eroding shores.

But why Proust? Why not
some obscure
14th century woman alone in her lab,
reading another woman
in fading light?

*Ruth Hubbard, 1924-2016*

## Dearest Mark

Dearest Mark, are we still on speaking terms
after that phone call echoing through time?
A stranger's voice pronouncing words I tried to erase
before they could take up residence in my ears.

Your giant heart exploding like calcium and rain,
tales of childhood in the bush
where rhinos challenged a queer storyline
and the road to your future stumbled.

Years, and I'm still angry you left so abruptly.
Not angry at you but at a world
where death devours without warning
and we are abandoned to the silence of suspense.

Zeus-like body preened and groomed,
feet that ran double marathons
on the blood-soaked earth of your first home
and the convoluted byways of your second.

It isn't your body, but your mind: unfinished novel
and arguments that hold me in close embrace,
fingers braiding and unbraiding memory
through narrow crevices of shame.

In pain you combed those rebellious strands
matted with their slime of lies,
nurtured each to a rebirth banished by many,
understood by those willing to risk fictitious comfort.

You showed me love of oneself leaves space
for the presence of friends if they can listen
to their own truth. I hesitated, then said yes
and never looked back except in this vastness of wanting.

*Mark Behr, 1963-2015*

## Dearest Laurette

Dearest Laurette, more than friend
you were mother and sister,
the chosen kind:
diminutive body, painful history,
playful intuitive mind.

It was that intuition the experts
in your field couldn't abide,
attacking you as woman and foreigner,
ignoring or disqualifying
what you heard in your head.

Transporting yourself in space
and time, you understood
human sacrifice unfiltered
by the cultural judgements of today,
standing outside our calendar.

Ghosts of other wars.
Ghosts of another war.
Other ghosts of war.
This or that ghost. This war now.
Always one more war.

Delicate gloved hands on the steering wheel
of your gray Peugeot,
wicker basket with roast chicken,
French bread and patés.
Our picnics at Teotihuacan.

War and ghost trains. A child lost
on a railway platform,
fascism beneath your fingernails
threatening
the freedom in your hair.

You married great men
but were never
consumed by them.
Your love affair with Quetzalcoatl
defied the elements.

You brought mystery to
dialectical materialism,
crosshairs that would
come into focus in a future
you didn't live to see.

I didn't understand half
of what you said
but your words charged my memory,
illuminated my growing,
shaped who I would become.

When your daughter confided
she'd stopped you
from ending your life
I was speechless with rage
and grief.

From you I learned that creative women
become their own ghosts,
will always be spurned
and must die to be heard,
accepted, recognized.

*Laurette Sejourné, 1911-2003*

## Dearest Felipe

Dearest Felipe, you were a man
large in art, grand gesture
entering a room, sucking
the air. We could only breathe
if we inhaled you.
I loved you despite yourself.

You produced beautiful children,
made new things,
exhibited a woman
whose creative brilliance shone
only after escaping
your furious orbit.

You married another goddess
but I doubt you stopped
bedding every woman who took
your fancy, that transgression
refined by the male
of our species.

I can imagine how vigorously
you fought the cancer
that took you, how you must have
brainwashed, bargained, bludgeoned,
hustled, coerced, and beaten it silly
in the night.

In death the edges of your body
seemed to push against
the confines of a coffin
that tried to contain your spirit
and your flesh. No use.
You won, if only by default.

*Felipe Ehrenberg, 1943–2017*

## Dearest Roque

Dearest Roque, you were never content
to record your life as it was,
reinvented yourself many times over,
disguising cartwheels in every line.

Supplanting an absent father, you claimed
ancestry from the Dalton gang,
adding America's Wild West to your legacy,
spirited horses running in your dreams.

Jesuit studies sent you over to the other side
and you joined your tiny country's
Communist party, age 14,
Little Boy Lost at weekly meetings.

There was your escape from the clutches
of the CIA when an earthquake split
the walls of your prison and you disappeared
into a religious procession passing by.

It's time you tell me which stories were true
and which you imagined as your script
passing from mouth to mouth
after you were gone.

Your philandering was legion but so was
your generosity and your mind. I like to
imagine the words you left in a woman's voice
were inspired by our debates.

I still hear you explaining what Vallejo meant
as you helped me birth the hardest crossover
of my life: age to reason,
meaning to the newness of sound.

When you went home to fight for freedom
in El Salvador, no one could have known
your own comrades would torture and kill you:
brutal volley to an ambushed heart.

Now every May 10th your almost 40 years
sink their teeth into wounds
that will not heal in my flesh:
too often betrayed, forever ready.

*Roque Dalton, 1935-1975*

## Dearest Maru

Dearest Maru, in your family the men
became princes of industry,
the women expected to marry
moneyed businessmen.
Your mother lived her best life
a president's concubine.

You were a sheep of a different color
or, rather, no sheep at all.
In Tai Chi grace
brightly embroidered shifts
hid your communist commitment
and fiercest courage.

I brought my infant son to Mexico
and you took us in hand.
We met when you taught him
third-grade English. Together
we fought every crude assault
and trickster's slight.

I move through memory and see us
hiding in your home,
repression of 1969.
My partner at the time, our four
small children and I
all gathered before a black and white TV

that July 20th, balancing dinner
on folding trays, we
watched a man step onto the moon.
Your husband fearing
our presence would bring trouble
and you defying his fear.

Soon after, you left that relationship,
spent the rest of your life alone
rather than cater to men
who would try to mold you
to their pleasure
and despair.

By the time you called to say goodbye,
our years of resistance,
lives of our making
had stretched to take others in.
We'd done enough
to make each other proud.

I asked if you were in pain.
No, you said, though
your words were worn velvet,
see-through and very soft.
The cancer had already won.
Two days later you were gone.

So much we shared never found
its way into complete sentences
but continues to burn:
dead embers in your eyes,
still glowing ones
waiting their turn in mine.

*Maru Uhthoff, 1937–2017.*

## Dearest Paul

Dearest Paul, it was hard to die
back when death
didn't enjoy its current range of action:
grabbed people right and left,
carried them off without warning.

They tell me you raged against
the cancer and I know
it must have been a struggle.
You had so much yet to dream,
to write, to do.

Translation wasn't common practice
when you brought Provençal
into English, surprised us
with Cortázar's *cronopios* and *famas*,
played games

with our minds beyond those poems
of your own that showed us
the city we lived in new to ear and eye:
that little girl moving fast
on the A train.

"Give the child words, give him/
words," you wrote, "and
he will use them." Simple as that.
Given the gift, you knew
how to pass it on.

Later I learned of the pictures you took
when I wasn't aware,
mementos you brought from Mexico
to my son's father
that he could trace the boy's life.

When I walk the streets of any
strange city I think of you,
filled with an energy
you would not live to use,
precious gifts we will never receive.


*Paul Blackburn, 1926–1971*

## Dearest Ceferino

Tough old guerrilla from the mountains
of Guerrero, member of
Genaro Vazquez's band,
fighting a nineteenth-century war
in twentieth-century Mexico.

Men on horseback with broken rifles
against a modern army,
no hope of victory,
vain faith giving you to believe
you had a chance.

Captured and imprisoned, you languished
for months until traded for
a Coca-Cola executive,
one kneecap putrid from the bullet
still lodged in bone.

Cuba received you as it did so many,
hastening to heal
the pain of misadventure
and scars of unequal war,
turning grief to dignity.

We met in the hospital where they
tended your physical wounds,
managed to get you walking again,

but I saw something else in your eyes:
a longing for hot chili on your tongue.

Over dishes spiced with a local *picante*
you told me of crossing the border,
following the lettuce
in a land that exploited
then tossed you out.

When you spoke of your father, I asked
"How old is he?" "About my age,"
you responded, and continued to tell me
of your family, oblivious your answer
made no sense.

I don't know what became of you.
Perhaps you found your way
back to a familiar landscape
though surely not the place
that was rightfully yours.

Magic realism, real as your strong
hands and toothless smile,
like so many whose innocence
rebukes those forced
to deny their dreams.

*Ceferino Contreras Ventura, 1917-1988*

## Dearest Kathy

Dearest Kathy, in a room with its furniture
bolted to the floor, prisoners and visitors
at cement tables, officer's eyes
forbidding us to touch.

No touching the vending machines either,
dehumanization the goal. I deposited
coins, bought paper cups of soup
and stale crackers wrapped in cellophane.

I also deposited memory in your hands,
as you in mine, knew you had
a life before, dreamed you might have one after.
Passionate talk. Passionate silences.

And you did have a life after those 22 years,
one you created from the friction
between control and hesitation, the unknown
bothering patience in your flesh.

Free, you rode your bike in Central Park,
worked tirelessly for those you left behind,
welcomed a grandchild to a world
where another opponent had you in its grip.

After struggles we cannot imagine, you left,
drying our tears on the way out,
one last conversation as you swallowed regret,
igniting. Igniting.

*Kathy Boudin, 1943–2022*

# Nepantla

*In memory of Gloria Anzaldúa,*
*1942-2004*

The space between is not always a borderland,
division between nations, origins,
even such aspects of being no longer
one or the other
but histories slammed together by rape,
cowering in fear, surviving
through the brilliance and cunning
of beings set on opposing journeys
finding a compromise they didn't seek.

Napantla separates two bodies of water
and also the death-defying drops
on either side of that narrow ridge
we humans walk
on this journey called living.
As the word rose on our ancestors' tongues
it ceased to describe only heritage,
warring factions or that melting pot
that is never what it pretends.

Living between cultures, ages, ideas
that say yes, we see double,
grasp magnets pulling us this way

and that, embrace
all that has fed us to now.
We celebrate change
as we experience ourselves
swinging back and forth, steady beat
of momentum, creative passion on fire.

Some know it as no-man's land,
a strip of earth
to keep warring visions of life apart,
a place that doesn't exist on any map
or hum in any key heard by those
imprisoned by time.
Then flowers began to grow, birds sing
and animals inhabit what we abandon
in our shame.

Some are born understanding Nepantla
runs through our bodies
and tend both sides as if they are gardens
of Eden. We know it is up to us
to choose which side lives and which dies,
spend years learning to ask
those questions that will keep us safe,
answers that will bring us
closer to ourselves.

Each of us holds that liminal reality
within, memory whispers

many names, we take what we need
or maybe what we can get
when both sides retreat from the middle,
battle lines imposed by bullies who possess
the largest fortunes, best technology,
lightest skin and most devious minds
used in pursuit of conquest.

Crossroads? That place where paths diverge
and we believe we must choose
one direction or another.
No. Never so easy or mundane.
Nepantla is the world the artist fills
with imagination, that space where we take
our ancestry in hand, use what we need,
discard what is harmful or superfluous,
speak our names.

What they cannot know because it has fled
their courtyard, left the premises
of collective knowledge, is that we,
the vanquished, carry nepantla in our flesh.
It is part of us, essence of how we feel
and move, where we go
taking that territory as a gift
to our children and children's children,
generations into a future we can only dream.

Nepantla is that place where multiple forms
of reality emerge simultaneously.
Sixteenth-century inhabitants
of Mexico's altiplano, invaded by the Spanish,
described an in-between
where they experienced slavery and resistance
moving through their veins,
call and response as old as the horror
humans inflict upon humans,

and new as tomorrow, gleaming as sun
on skin that has weathered
eons of land grabs, centuries of pain
suffered not in honor
but with the courage of a newborn
when she opens her eyes
and begins to learn
she will have to defend herself
against armies of entitlement.

The space between is not always a borderland
or even a puzzle's unfinished edge
crashing against another puzzle.
Nepantla is where we meet ourselves
when hope is dead
but tiny shoots of green emerge
from earth we must nourish with what we see
when we close our eyes
and reach back through history.

## When I Lived

When I lived, I passed through a place
inhabited by ghosts.
If you slow your step
you can feel them hiding
in their fancy clothes among the trees.

My shadow remains in that place,
retreating midday
and stretching its lonely arms
in early morning and late afternoon
as it sings offkey to itself.

Those who find themselves there by chance
may feel my presence, the nudge
of my elbow or smoldering of my desire,
may hear the rustle of my words
caught in the highest branches.

But those who seek out that place
as destination
receive complete sentences, a music
beyond their imagination, a certainty
in the quickening of their pulse.

Danger shows itself in many disguises,
plays a rough game
and gives you to know that only risk
will take you where you want to go,
leaving your name as cairn.

# Geode

You need a hammer and strong hand
to split this lump of gray rock
hiding its crystal beauty, a world
where geology's heart takes you
into its wonder.

It is nature's piñata, shining star
deeper and more hidden
than that shower of candy and trinkets
giving way to the birthday child's
final blow.

I would crawl inside it if I could,
curl my body into its mystery:
roam its billions of years,
become one with the energy
of its desire.

# Back to Front or Inside Out

Neither political nor pastoral
because the brushstroke
is broad, the paint
still wet and glistening.

Not a how-to manual because
the instructions can be read
in any order, back
to front or inside out.

No list or table of contents
with items to be added
or subtracted
according to whim, one by one.

Nor an outline with points
to be fleshed out
as sunrise extends
your line of sight.

The poem happens on its own
terms, no rules dragging
behind: the proverbial
tail between its legs.

It arrives upright, full-throated,
and you must get
out of its way,
let it take shape and shout.

## My Father's Eyes

As he left, his eyes led the way:
receding films, distant
and tired, sinking into an armature
of dying flesh.

My father was kind and gentle,
refusing to reedit
his own progenitor's
cold disdain.

Dad saw good everywhere
and sang its chorus
though liberation never embraced him
while he lived.

As his eyes disappeared
into slowing eddies
I imagined them opening wide
on another shore,

spreading again to contain
a pulsing ocean
in a place where unquestioning love
would be his.

## Becoming Ourselves

Where we go next depends upon a landscape
etched by wind.

Color sings, a golden sax paints purple
on orange cliffs.

Climbing or descending, brown spars with green
behind our eyes.

Clashing childhood stories send us
in different directions.

Becoming ourselves, we begin to move
toward one another.

Promises sing anthems
in our veins.

Temperature is a magnet in bodies
that yearn.

Now we are closer to the exit
than the launch

and the questions still weigh more
than the answers.

Where we go next depends upon a landscape
etched by wind.

## All Those Years Ago

Have you ever wondered
what a simple change,
say for example your teacher
all those years ago
greeting the class
*good morning girls and boys*
instead of *boys and girls,*
might have done
for your
self-esteem?

Have you ever imagined
blue—electric or sky,
seafoam or periwinkle
or any of the radiant shades
morphing to purple
as it flees navy—
rather than that insipid pink
absorbing your breath
and giving nothing back?

Is it too late to undo
every assumption,
each alluring prescription
stamped and sealed
in its glittering wrapper,

seduction its weapon
as it wrings you dry
one infinitesimal turn
of the screw at a time?

Are you able to step away,
look back or down,
as the case may be,
and take a quiet breath?
Changed expectation
offers a changed reality
as surely as opening a window
invites fresh air
into a musty room.

Notice the bridge. It will
encourage you
to walk across.
Accept that the thunderhead
may bring a wall of mud
or tumbling branches
along with refreshing rain.
It is part of the risk
and its promise is everything.

## My Theory of Nothing

They are excited by a *Theory of Everything*,
gravity to the tiniest sub-particle
of cosmic dust,
something to explain where we come from,
where we are going
and what we have learned
along the way.

Like a giant jigsaw, the placid lake
assembles easily
but its shore is still torn by empty spaces
and the surrounding mountains
are missing gaping holes
yet to be filled. We cannot see
the connections.

I am searching for a Theory of Nothing,
not explanation
so much as remedy
for all that is wrong
with this system and its million
grasping claws tearing our limbs
from hunger.

My pot of gold at the end of a neon rainbow
beckons with a smile,

snuggles up to the passion
hiding in a nearby poem
or the rich earth
young children turn over
with toy shovels.

Those guys in their garments of privilege
share a grand goal, ambition
trampling community gardens
in an age when patriarchy
keeps the big prizes
for the fast food
musketeers.

But Everything shivers this bleak
winter night,
asks how we imagine
the infinite and infinitesimal
can inhabit the same sentence.
For once they find themselves
out in the cold.

A Theory of Nothing folds me
into its arms,
murmurs secrets that fill the silences
they endeavor to protect.
*Remedy, please*, I repeat,
as I move from sleep
to grasp the nearest hand.

## The Sum of One and One

The earth was barren,
battered by centuries
of greed
and salt of abandon.

The poet insisted on planting a word,
nurturing its hesitant roots
and dreaming the rain
that would bring it life.

That single word grew lonely
at times, dependent
on the poet's
nurturing memories.

Once the word stood strong
on its windswept home
the poet planted
another.

She taught them collaboration
and that the sum of
one and one is always
more than two.

Time passed and returned
with unexpected gifts.
A field of words reaches for
meaning among the weeds.

The words are a poem now,
its rhythms piercing
a million ears crowding close
that they may hear.

## Understanding Metaphor

Without a sense of humor about
where Jesus was baptized
when warring countries claim the spot,

without understanding metaphor
when it comes to raising the dead
or that production line of bread and fish,

without the patience to follow a darkling beetle
on its labored journey through sand
or watch the dance as light and shadow

switch places in a picture-perfect landscape
as night descends and dreams
fill the canyons behind your eyes,

you may have become a handmaiden
without noticing privilege
is gone for good.

## When I Die

When I die if you speak of me
at all please say I am dead.
Do not use phrases like
*transitioned* or *passed on*
or describe me as
moving toward the light.

I never lived in darkness
although darkness
often came knocking at my door
trying to lure me
onto its path
of lazy impersonation.

I always resisted, stumbled and
fell but picked myself up,
brushed deceptive lies
from denim pants
and steadied my breath
for the journey ahead.

I want to know death
as I knew life:
full throttle and conscious
of its idiosyncrasies,
as uniquely mine as
my chosen culture prescribes.

We may comfort ourselves
with fantasies
that calm our spirits,
warm our fearful minds.
Truth is my faithful lover,
balm for every doubt.

Still, you may be surprised
to know my certainty
also possesses its quota
of magic,
landscape of wonder
in cosmic energy.

# Never the Compliment it Pretends

*For all those who are forced from their homes*
*by terror or want and never completely*
*arrive in the promised land.*

*Where you from?* the fine edge of a razorblade
beneath your nails or an innocent question
hiding behind the clown's sad mask—greasepaint
smudged as it leers its happy face.

The immigrant pronounces her country's name
in almost perfect English. She's practiced
before a mirror in which she struggles
to find herself.

The questioner may turn away or say *that's nice*
or tell her she doesn't look like people
from there, which is never the compliment
it pretends.

Hollywood's promise turns faded celluloid
at a neighborhood cineplex
where the smell of stale popcorn
clings to her thrift shop garb.

And the person who endured years of paperwork
or crossed beneath the cover of night

is no longer from there and will never
completely be here.

She remembers the texture of rain, waves beating
against a broken sea wall, feel of air
on her face or that homegrown hardship
familiar to her hands.

Those memories grow distant as the years unfold
and her daughter's distant eyes
greet her when she tells the stories
she keeps beneath her pillow.

# Desert

Wind writes its autobiography in sand,
mummified mesquite sap
inking millennial rock, turning
dry riverbeds to intimate history.

Wild English gardens may tilt their heads
and lift their aristocratic chins
enveloped in the watery fog
of nurturing rains.

The French cut their hedges
in perfect shapes,
patterning nature to reflect
their sense of reason.

Here the fuchsia blossoms on a cholla
cling resolutely to its withered arm,
proud agaves flower once
every decade.

On deserts the welwitschia with its two
lonely leaves or bristlecone pine
are the exclamation points
moving the story past sage and cedar.

Giant trunks of ancient trees turn
to agate, their petrified colors
waiting to be washed by the next
great flood or future sea.

Canyon walls lick voluptuous lips of fire
where color explodes
to the rhythms of a disappearing sun
that leaves no heat behind.

Patience is required to read this memoir
of life and death, eons of beauty
at a single hungry glance
on a canvass too vast to digest.

# The Acequias

The acequias are dry, dust blowing
where water once ran;
alfalfa lies desiccate, corn stalks
bear sad ears, blighted kernels.

The news came first in sweeping
predictions: photos of cracked earth,
heat-deformed plastic bottles,
graphs of sinking water tables.

Then neighbors spoke of dying farms,
their losses touching you
where regret pinches your flesh
with its bony fingers.

This morning you turn the handle
above your sink and nothing
issues from the spigot
but the hiss of parched regret.

Meanwhile, a multi-billion dollar
space program announces
the discovery of water on Mars
in small but promising quantities.

## Water's Desire

Scientists now believe
they've discovered
water has memory,

each drop containing
its unique pattern
resulting

from where it has been
what moves it forward
and what it carries.

Water speaks, telling
its own story
of pain or desire.

My tears are encyclopedic,
bursting with absence,
loss and the joy

that overflows reason.
They make their way
down the ravines of my face.

Their memories chew the meat
on my bones as they dry
and wait to feed another season.

# Ode to Typography

*For Rafael Mondragón*

"Writing begins with the making of footprints,
the leaving of signs. Like speaking, it is a
perfectly natural act which humans have carried
to complex extremes. The typographer's task
has always been to add a somewhat unnatural
edge, a protective shell of artificial order, to the
power of the writing hand. The tools have altered
over the centuries, and the exact degree of
unnaturalness desired has varied from place to
place and time to time, but the character of the
essential transformation between manuscript
and type has scarcely changed. "[2]

"Instinct . . . is largely memory in disguise."[3]

—Robert Bringhurst

They knew about form and content,
those designers of type
with their modulated strokes, variable axes
and lachrymal terminals.
With or without serifs: medieval, gothic,
baroque, renaissance, classic or postmodern,

---

2      *The Elements of Typographic Style*, 18.
3      Ibid, 144.

they created letters with memories
and strong backbones
ready to make a home for words.

Their font styles shouted or whispered,
sometimes laughed out loud
or sang harmony to a melody
that pressed against the heart
with the strength of forever conviction.
Dangerous secrets fail to thrive
in lettering that knows its place
but will also cross
restrictive lines.

And then there are the innocent secrets
inviting us to games of fantasy.
They may be hiding in plain sight
or require some knowledge of the journey
to reveal themselves,
take us on a passage of discovery
through the words we believe
issue without echo
in our minds.

Font designers were men of rules, and most
were men. I only found a woman or two
among the legion of names.
But their rules extended only as far
as rationale would take them.

These were artists of quiet passion
and balance, and the foundries rang
with the sound of metal bent over anvils
where imagination left its print.

In Athens and Rome, the modulated stroke
and bilateral serif were symbols
of empire, Sans Serif's
unmodulated forms
spoke for people's resistance
to autocratic rule, cultural souvenirs
of bright periods in human history
when chains were broken
to forge the letters that invite us in.

History told by those who made it
instead of the conquering hero
demands an austere letter,
simple font to give it weight.
A poem written in minor key
may benefit from the mystery
of shapes reminiscent
of an ancient script, unreadable
by anyone alive today.

Tall letters, chorus of downstrokes
in perfect verticals
aren't millennial trees
reaching for the sky

but tell a story
that will take your breath away.
It is the forest and also the trees
speaking through and around
our words.

Less is more when deciding
the aperture of a C or M,
circumference of an O
or how a Y drags its injured leg.
Superfluous tangles or twists
may enhance moments of doubt
but steady equilibrium endures
when dignity's pride
is at stake.

In perfect reach, a letter may lean
a degree or two to the right,
another will shift its interior weight
simulating an angle
while you close one eye and imagine
a vessel of old sailing into the wind
and veering off course, a horse
bucking its rider or the Tower of Pisa
resisting gravity all these years.

Analphabetic symbols such as periods,
commas, colons, and semicolons,
exclamation points and question marks,

asterisks or dashes of varying widths
differ from typeface to typeface
always trying to maintain the elegance
for which a named design
claims its place in the history
of script.

Italics and bold, Roman, and Arabic
pull me from sleep
with a mood to meet the day.
I am Jerónimo Antonio Gil in Mexico City
cutting an Otomí language font in 1785
or Carol Twombly mid 20th century New York,
lone woman among men
creating tilting faces with names
like Lithos, Charlemagne, Nueva, Viva.

In this age of little yellow smiley faces,
pulsing hearts and other emoticons,
Baskerville, Bodoni, Caslon,
Electra, Garamond, Helvetica, Palatino,
Futura and all their kind
are the calm before the storm.
Patience is their virtue,
risk their alter ego, a place
where critical thought stops and waves.

We have gone from chiseled stone
to forged alloy, from handset

to linotype, then photographic methods
and the digital techniques we use today,
each vying for cost-effective labor ease
while maintaining the elegance
of its noble history,
all based on the human body:
eye, hand, and forearm.

*This is an artform unique to our species,*
the historian tells us, *dogs and ants*
*read and write by more chemical means.*
Scribes, artists, scholars, calligraphers,
architects, typographers, astronomers,
mathematicians, engravers, poets, and printers
have all given us this lettered history
responding to the eager mind
and fingertips of those who see in darkness.

We are talking about pica, not pixels,
breathing the shape of letters,
a history of type that is a map
of writing we explore on foot
that we may touch the space
each letter claims and the distance
in between: the sculptural image
giving form to our meaning
and content to our form.

# Footprints

*Again, for Raul Zurita*

I am writing these words I want readers
to understand
are about my final days.

There's no indication my end is imminent
but at eighty-five
no guess can take a chance.

Searching for new blooms, I cast out the weeds
and water earth
as parched and dry as failing skin.

Remembering where I stumbled and fell,
glimmers of hope
sprout wings on a landscape of witness.

Writing about the end before arriving at the end
is like remembering
a color photograph in black and white.

You created a glyph etched in Atacama sand
and made of words one can only view
from the sky.

Mine is the small story of a woman hounded
by gender and place
where risk came down on survival's side.

I implore them: stop talking now, listen
in silence to where I am going,
no destination assured.

Trust my memory, what I have seen and felt,
footprints left to be discovered
when life passes this way again.

# The Hole in Your Calendar

*For Barrett*

Your calendar of important dates,
sad ones and joyous, hovers
beyond that page where eraser force
ripped a hole in memory
calculated to weather any storm.

Those 20 minutes of death
are like a coat hanger
without your old jeans jacket
worn by living,
familiar to your skin.

A space where memory has
no foothold. No matter
how hard it tries
it cannot catch up with itself
or rock you back to sleep.

And sleep itself is at risk, you are
only in synch with yourself
when you can hear the steady beat
of your ancient drum
rising this side of emptiness.

Emptiness always corrodes
but when you are
emptied of self you must
guard your limbs and feed your mind
a soil-rich balm.

Newborn once more, you carry
a lifetime of loving,
recognition and escape.
Then milepost zero surprises you
at the trail's edge.

It's those missing minutes, precisely 20,
that invade your dreams
without invitation, those questions
whose answers are writ
in disappearing ink.

Returning from temporary death
risk repeats itself like minutes
that keep sounding
beyond the finish line, an itch
you cannot scratch.

New life may take your hand
but loss continues
to whisper and call,
telling you stories in a language
you struggle to learn.

You must make peace with
the abyss,
that time when you weren't
leaving you trembling
in present tense.

Echo is your worthy opponent now.
It may threaten to appear
when you least expect its vibrations
to trouble the thinnest membrane
or nestle easily in your palm.

# Dubious Gifts

*For Leandro Katz*


Animal noises live within us even as Disney
replaces them with voiceover cackles,
erasing nature's memory, playing
for an audience of millions.

Our sons and brothers come with the dubious gift
of *want* translated ritualistically as *need*
or *demand*. We try to help them see the danger
even as they force entry in our flesh.

And we, so often called the weaker sex, are also born
owing a debt that can't be paid except by traveling
obstacle courses strewn with body parts
in the rain-soaked earth of killing fields.

We used to believe only in us and them, a concept
we applied to trust, the art of bullying
or the win we accrue by stealing another's water,
tilling another's field.

Defining sex or gender by traditional binary rules
puts freedom off limits or confines it to a zoo
where the mother lion sings a story of vast savannah
to its bewildered young.

In our youth we thought we could subvert those strictures
by ingesting entheogens: Mexican mushroom,
bitter peyote button, or drink. We were left with the filmstrip
flapping on a projector crowing to the void.

With age it's memory we harness to perform the whole script
in lives where poetry is our language,
landscape our imagination, and justice the only
rule we care to keep.

## Not Even the Cheetah

This race to say it all before the finish line
heats up and I worry there's
no more time for words, the poem
you hear before I open my mouth.

Half tortoise but not half hare, maybe
cheetah: the fastest animal.
At times I outrace myself and at others
notice everything in my path.

I must choose between two cadences,
two directions, an option
that wedges itself between my left cheek
and shoulder

like a violin that asks to be played
by the virtuoso who hides
her panic attacks
beneath her pillow at night.

Not a matter of dueling personalities,
hesitation or days when
everything breaks,
mine is a curious arc.

I want to say it all before my journey
fizzles and breathes its last.
But if I can't, no one will be the wiser,
not even the cheetah.

# From *Home*

Abiquiu, New Mexico: Casa Urraca Press 2023

## This Home on My Back

Some people live in the same house
their whole lives. Mother may
make a brief hospital detour
then bring baby back to rooms whose
shapes she's known all hers.

They will grow, raise their families
and die between those walls.
Trees they helped plant when young
now tower above its roofline,
dropping new seed upon the ground.

My houses embrace me after accidental
journeys. I sometimes had to exit fast
or take a dangerous route, learning
the words *underground* and *clandestine*
in languages I didn't know.

My gardens, when I could plant them,
grew annuals not perennials,
knowing I might have to leave
before I could encourage their return
another season.

In my attic there is no cedar-lined chest
storing remnants of forebears' lives,

no family albums with photos
arranged in chronological memory
or books my mother's mother read to her.

My children didn't have the chance
to know their grandparents,
had no aunts and uncles taking them
to the park, cousins tossing them
a ball or telling family secrets.

I've carried my life from country
to country in small knapsacks
on my back, crossed borders with
choked breath, hoping ominous uniforms
would look the other way.

The food I cook isn't traditional
but learned in each new place,
glimmers of solidarity trading hands
over stoves that use whatever fuel
is to be had.

Age, a steady love, and this era
of slowing rhythms
make its own home for me now,
one in which all those
imagined disappear.

Oh, but the people we've met
along the way, the dreams
and ideas and poems they've
given us, the justice reflected
in their eyes!

The home I bequeath my children
and grandchildren isn't made
of stone or brick but moves like wind
in your hair, carrying its energy
across all borders into future time.

# Home as Oxymoron

From outside looking in
every house might be
called a home.

But if the child is frightened
into submission she is
only there until she escapes.

If forced to parent her parents
she may not remember
childhood.

If he was told to be a man
he may grow up to be
a brutal one.

When family becomes cult
home is an oxymoron
dangerously hoarded.

To become a real home, it
must earn its name
in reciprocity and love.

## The Shame no Wearable Can Erase

This house wears a beige trench coat,
the kind with upturned collar
and loosely knotted belt
showing a lean and hungry body, revolver
holstered but at the ready.

A Maasai hut, constructed of cow dung
and anthill soil, wraps the vivid red
of a Sears blanket above its loin cloth
as it goes in search of the trail
of lion scent.

In the far north, an ice-block igloo
protects itself against the cold
with whale blubber, seal skins and a parka
guaranteed by L.L. Bean to withstand
up to 50 degrees below.

Men cover the heads and bodies of
their fundamentalist homes
in hair or wig or heavy cloth, possession
nine-tenths of the law. The home cries
silent obedience.

A starter home buys cotton sundresses
each spring, ruffle and flounce,

hasn't yet learned more elegant outfits
straddle the seasons
and remain in fashion.

The old commune shopped *vintage* when
*vintage* and *used* meant the same.
Now *used* has raised its margin of profit
and *vintage* is the Stradivarius
only a virtuoso can afford.

The rooms added onto this house
bare their midriffs in summer
but cover their windows
with lace curtains replacing truth
with memory's lies.

An expensive retreat in its gated community
flaunts jewels and ostentatious furs,
Jimmy Choo heels and
the $5000-dollar evening bag:
subtle as glamorous.

A penthouse dons the most expensive suit,
imported Italian serge and tailoring
only mega bucks can buy, except when it
settles on a personal trademark:
turtleneck, black.

Any one of the rent-controlled apartments
in these projects, elevator
reeking of piss, would rather its children
wear school uniforms
than see its men in prison green.

I know a house where overalls hide a body
afraid of being touched,
although the latest shoes and bags
bring a sense of self
it can't resist.

My own home wears Levi's and a black shirt,
short sleeves in summer, long in winter,
rarely changes for any occasion.
It is statement, not necessity,
message rather than style.

The man or woman who has no home
shuffles through the streets
in a ragged blanket or whatever they find.
Style loses its importance
when all it covers is need.

Each house appears in clothes
designed to do their best
against the demands of industry,
transformation, or
the shame no wearable can erase.

# The Great Houses, Chaco[4]

*For my grandson, Eli Bickford*


We call it the Menefee formation,
this peach-colored sandstone
rising in billowing benches,
shouldering eighty million years.

Reflecting all that summer sun,
its bulk and crevices dance
in our eyes, imposing monument
upon a land that holds its secrets close.

Beside them, the great houses
hewn from this rock bear
no evidence anyone lived in
their hundreds of small dark rooms.

No blackened walls, few hearths
from cooking fires confirming
daily life, no middens ripe
with household debris.

---

4   I've visited Chaco Canyon many times over the years, but a recent
visit—immediately after viewing Anna Sofaer's 1999 film "The Mys-
tery of Chaco Canyon"—provided me with a deeper understanding
of the site that is reflected in this poem.

This is an intimate grandeur
immense as the fingertips
of two lovers meeting in a city
neither knows.

Living rock dies in these chiseled blocks
yet it isn't dead but has become
the liminal space time's transition
sets before us.

The great kivas are roofless now.
Only ghosts dance within,
perpetuating their meaning,
guarding their secrets.

Mounds of broken pottery
tell stories of offerings
made in rituals hidden
beyond our consciousness.

Built on this hard scrabble earth,
standing four or five stories
tall, their broken silhouettes
weather seasons and centuries.

Even at midday, long shadows pass
in angular movement
framing windows of sky, puffs of cloud
in depths of blue.

Traveling from the four directions,
the people found this center,
hauled rock and timber to align
the cosmos in this place.

For generations they recorded cycles
of sun and moon, traced
an accurate astronomical signature
in ceremonial memory.

I almost close my eyes and a dish-
shaped moon becomes
lunar repetition moving in tandem
across the night.

I imagine an adolescent girl, perhaps
thirteen or fourteen, walking
the Great North Road from her people
far to the south.

Her garment is loose, her hair black
and braided. She carries
knowledge and intention
to this land on which

every eighteen-and-a-half-year cycle
the moon casts a dagger of light:
its perfect image piercing the spiral
etched on rock.

Today's celestial body shines upon
this barren and desolate landscape,
offering the same light
it did back then.

The girl still walks through time,
one step before another,
measuring where we've been
and where we have yet to go.

Leaving no written language,
architecture and location
is their script. Past meets future
in the old man's eyes

as he tells us: *parts of that story*
*aren't meant to be told,*
*those parts where the power*
*gleaned by some*

*may have caused certain things*
*to happen, wrong turns*
*to be taken or mistakes that*
*needn't be repeated.*

*Their knowledge may have*
*been too great,* he says,
*and something changed,*
*went bad.*

Knowing we do not need to know
it all may seem a misstep of faith
but things were different then.
They faced the same uncertainty

we battle today but their imaginations
took root in a landscape
whose voices spoke to them.
They listened.

## Nothing but Need at their Side

They tell great stories about their childhood homes:
hers on the prominent shore of a placid lake
surrounded by other monied families, his smaller one
nurtured by his teacher parents. He brought the politics
they embody to the life they share.

Honoring gay friends who couldn't marry back then,
they never did so either. Their son bears
her surname because, why not? The children
whose families shared their floorspace and dreams
were his brothers and sisters.

As young professors they lived in an old three-story
collective house, shared kitchen, cooked meals
together and navigated its communal spaces.
They parented intentionally and laughed
when friends asked about their way of life.

The commune was always their goal, and they lived
that goal beyond the walls that held them
city to city as they grew in their professions,
moved from one college town to another until
they settled in this desert sun.

Their one-family home is filled with art from
the Navajo family she studied for decades,

is lined with his books on Brazil's economy.
It stretched to make five years of room
for the first Begay to go beyond high school,

an old friend who needed a roof for years
and now their son, his wife and child,
because extended family is also where
he feels comfortable and what he wants
his daughter to inherit.

Which is why we are bereft of words when
they tell us they are moving
to *assisted living*, eldercare with a *memory unit*
in case he forgets how they used to live
and what it meant.

*It has a beautiful view of the mountains*, she
explains, *and chances are one of us
will need the help as we grow older.*
Hiding our tears, we take a last look around,
smile and nod our heads,

trying to imagine *assisted living* as a new kind
of commune, capitalism's answer to human
frailty for those who have the means
while others try to survive on streets
with nothing but need in their hands.

## A Different Language

My curiosity sometimes retreats
to decades before my birth
and I watch a distant European relative
turn down an unfamiliar street.

This prevents her from running
into the man she married,
alters her life completely, thus
cancelling or replacing mine.

One small difference, a day that turned
stormy rather than bright,
accidents or choices made by those
we never knew.

A desire to speak silenced by sudden
shame. A piece of music perfectly
performed, leading to an outcome
challenging history.

The rogue gene, brazen decision,
fear hiding in plain sight
or courage rising on a tide
that switches direction in the night.

The insult that cannot be forgotten,
a child lost at war's end, one face
missing or added to
from a family photograph.

Good fortune embraced her for a while,
then didn't. He was said to have
a way with women until his wife
chose death rather than one more day.

She became the woman she always
knew she was. He refused
to give in to his entitlement, forfeited
confidence to social equanimity.

The storm of the century, the one
they called perfect. Famine
eroding teeth and muscle, generosity
or arrogance stealing the scene.

Ordinary or extraordinary events
in ordinary lives. The lie
that prospered or a truth
that could not speak its name.

Any one of those choices allowed,
provoked, stumbled upon
this future that is me. And I cannot
but wonder about another story,

one in which I was born somewhere
else, spoke a different language,
am taller, healthier, darker of skin
or don't exist at all.

# Their Houses

Their houses still pretend
to be their homes,
price of a ticket to explore
rooms cordoned off
to excessive curiosity.
And we tickle an illusion
of how they lived.

I could barely stand in
Cady Stanton's
bedroom, couldn't
imagine a mattress
large enough to hold
her solid bulk, the desk
that framed her passion.

Elvis's mansion displays
the pomp and glitter
needed to hide
the insecurity
beneath his swivel-
hipped gyrations
and magnificent voice.

Searching for the General's
final home
in a northern field
where she was free,
I found no historic evidence,
no sign proclaiming
*Harriet Tubman Lived Here.*

O'Keeffe's spartan rooms
give us a low bench here,
sun-bleached cow skull
there, tell us loud and clear
we may not cross
the line she drew
while alive.

Frida, always more flamboyant,
hid her withered leg
but bared
a vibrant heart
and Plaster of Paris bodice.
Her ashes greet us from
the pillow where she died.

Ho Chi Minh resided
in two rooms
even when president,

had to walk a block
to a bathroom.
His modesty
still inspires.

Mandela returned
from his years
in prison to the same
simple house
on the same street
where he lived
before that arduous test.

And there's Queen Elizabeth II,
longest reigning monarch
in a nation where some
resent her palaces
while many still feel
their own lives brightened
by the pomp of royalty.

Some houses of those
we admire from afar
woo us with their books
or copper kitchen pots:
Hemingway's typewriter,
the post-it notes
stuck to Leonora's stove.

The houses we visit
hoping to inhale
the air our idols breathed,
the lives they lived,
are only absent
of the men and women
who inhabited them.

## If Forced to Go

If I had to pack an emergency bag
to have at the ready in event
of fire or flood, I would have to include
the big wall with your painting of swings,
one hundred books and this table
that welcomes friends to food
and conversation.

It would be hard to do without
our bed, that soft place
where I soiled a sheet in fever
and you washed it without a word,
where your nervous legs
eventually settle into
restful sleep,

scene of the love we make
and that which simply
surrounds and holds us
in its arms, aroused and safe
at the same time,
that place we belong
and that belongs to us.

My emergency bag would have
to be large enough to hold

this house with its hidden places
vast and small, all memories
past and present,
all objects solid and incorporeal
I'd want to take if forced to go.

## Adobe Dreams

Adobe dreams the heat of ancient summers
before earth worried a future
now breaking down all doors,
crawling through every open window.

Like those igloos carved from arctic ice,
home grows from what is:
place as possibility. Paper stretched across
a bamboo frame in Japanese restraint,

bison skins on the Great American Plains,
Iroquois Longhouse or Bucky's
geodesic dome. Highrise, penthouse,
tract, or starter home.

Ndebele's brightly painted abodes talk back
to a history of slavery's dismal canvass.
When Wright and Colter used local materials
it wasn't economy but elegance of vision,

oneness with a horizon that embraces
its settlers generously. From the cluster
of tents where those without homes
make do to a movement

of Tiny Homes where less is more
because it can be. *People who live*
*in glass houses shouldn't throw stones* isn't
about what we use to build our cocoons

but how we act once we dwell in them,
infusing our shelter with the energy
of each breath drawn, each word or gesture
that makes a house a home.

# What I Harvest

Morning opens its sleep-filled eyes,
deposits pink and orange
between the dark slats of
my bedroom blind, still closed
to resist the day.

If I raise the shade, this wall changes
from artichoke to lettuce green
and I notice the surfaces
are painted a progression
of hues.

Such range of light raises
the temperature
of my mind, these hours
I've spent on an idea as old
as primal data.

Winter's frozen arms reach out
to pull me into its cave
of icicles, stalagmites
bruising my body with
their crooked fingers of pain.

The greens work as intended, wake
to keep me safe, hold me apart

from a world I don't want,
won't invite in or visit
in these treacherous times.

It's all about intensity of color,
slowed breath coming
to the rescue, planting its seed
at the hollow of my throat
and what I harvest there.

# Homeless

*Homeless* we call them, as if
the designation carries
all that they are: those without
homes in this richest country,
sleeping in doorways
or seeking refuge in shelters
with more demand than beds.

Our language is so often
too small in this way,
names people for what
they lack rather than
the human complexity
that fills us all: identities
that do us proud.

*Homeless* we say, instead
of *those without*
*a home at present,* who
had one once and may
have one again if luck
and aid conspire to change
direction in their lives.

We live in a culture that defines
existence at its worst,

shies away from the
empathy that would let us
see wholeness beyond
that moment in time
when tragedy strikes its blow.

# What We Can Pretend We Do Not See

From the outskirts of town
you can see 100 miles
on a clear day, no smoky air
lying in wait
to override the view.

On the fringes, smaller homes
wander along dirt roads
needing windows, a door,
and other improvements
only money can buy.

The childless couple with
a home on the hill
pays someone to clean
their empty bedrooms, change
the water in their pool.

The immigrant family shares
two bedrooms
with cousins who made it
across a barbed wire border
fleeing thirst and dogs.

The home that gnaws at my conscience
is no home at all

but a dangerous street
where weather and violence
assault by turns.

Ours is a belligerent architecture
of property and taunt:
what we are willing to look at
and what we can pretend
we do not see.

# Faked Orgasms and Beloved Books

A bedroom no longer remembers
faked orgasms or beloved books
read by lamplight on a night table
bathed in memorabilia.

Living room has lost its portraits
of family gatherings, evenings
meant to impress a boss
or hide a high school kiss.

Kitchen has forgotten its favorite
recipes. Too little salt in the
soup, excess of sugar
coating the tongue with regret.

Studio's hand trembles now when
it tries to apply paint to paper,
its writer's mind believes it will find
the lost word but doesn't.

Fireplace mantel cannot name
the trophies once parading
across its polished wood,
boasting triumph over will.

Even the attic, accustomed to boxes
of keepsakes stored for a rainy day,
has forgotten what lives
in its corners, carries its name.

Front door cannot say who entered
here, back door doesn't recall
who left. This house struggles
with dementia, tries hard

to pretend *it's all good*, rehearses
its answers, hoping those
who live between its walls
won't abandon its loving arms.

# Non-Negotiable

My home is a cavern of heartbeats
scaling its innermost walls
like a rock climber placing his toes
in ancient cracks.

My home is an ocean of slave ships
and shipwrecks but also
dolphins and whales
cresting the waves.

My home is rich in questions, forged
by the wonder of each generation
as it takes its place
at the table.

My home considers *need to know*
when it talks to me,
teaches me the power of patience
and resilience.

My home says shame is the only thing
it will not allow to cross
its threshold. *Non-negotiable*, it says,
and folds its arms.

## This Table

This table's polished pine
remembers a forest
where young men and women
hide behind massive trunks:
Davids facing Goliath.

I set its surface with dishes
also hewn from the earth,
place forks to the left
of each setting, knives
and spoons to the right.

I ask the table to support elbows
of family and friends,
food in its daily rhythm,
conversation about that war
closing in on our home.

When the staccato of gunfire
and moans of the dying
are at a distance we believe
ourselves safe. The table
knows nothing and everything

about war, inequality, and grief,
trade routes that take
more than they give
and celebrate survival
only once every choice is spent.

# From *Your Answer is Your Map*

Green River, Vermont: Bob & Susan Arnold's Longhouse, 2023

Margaret Randall

*Your Answer Is Your Map*

Longhouse
*Publishers & Booksellers*
Green River, Vermont
© 2023 Margaret Randall
Photographs & Poems

*Staircase*, Tunis, Tunisia
*Keet Seel*, Arizona
*Windmill*, Tinos, Cyclades
*Ranchos de Taos Church*, New Mexico
*Broken Arch*, Ramesseum, Egypt
*Temple of Literature Doors*, Hanoi, Vietnam
author's photo by Pascual Borzelli
www.LonghousePoetry.com
9 *of 100*

## Our Progress is Plastic and Cement


We measure and name our era
Holocene, drawing a line
beginning 11,700 years in the past
when that terrifying ice melted.
We call its surviving humans primitive,
imagine grunts, fire as prize, raw meat
and chance discoveries.

The experts stoke religious denial,
biblical time and progress
as superiority, describe a people
without history or written language
to bequeath us a narrative
of barely intelligent life, not a Shakespeare
or Mozart among them.

Atop Fajada Butte at the ceremony
that is Chaco Canyon,
we watch the dagger of light
split in perfect halves that spiral
carved on rock, note how each
Great House is aligned with a planet
and begin to unravel the lie.

Then we learn it's not only Chaco
but ancient sites across the globe:

stone circles and mounds of earth
giving lie to our supremacy.
Ego of race and gender preceded by
that great ego of civilized man: a weight
we nurture shamelessly.

Studies not born of a single life
spent chasing the big prize
but centuries of observation.
Calendars that challenge the accuracy
of atomic time. Earth, sky,
and the human body stitched together
in a poetry of waiting.

Our progress is plastic and cement
clogging oceans, debris of all sorts
cluttering space. We turn our backs
on the energy of sun and wind,
rape the earth of its most vulnerable bounty,
invade and kill to stockpile a future
destroyed before it arrives.

Our academy praises such sophistication,
reaps billions in profit, while
the 300,000 inhabitants of tiny Vanuatu
ask if anyone cares their nation
is disappearing beneath a rising sea
in a future too close for comfort
or solution.

*We were here*, those ancestral voices
tell us, *but you didn't listen,*
*couldn't hear our stories,*
*honor our knowledge or the rhythm*
*of a wisdom that doesn't fit*
*this conviction you sustain*
*with your entitlement.*

# The Cranes are Coming

The cranes are coming,
floating on currents
of polluted air,
settling in fields of grain,
strutting their end-of-winter stuff.

Some cross the Bering Straits
every spring and fall,
enroute from nesting grounds
as distant as Siberia,
fearing no line of demarcation.

Sandhills in purposeful migration
to southern wetlands,
hundreds of thousands will winter
along our southern border,
no papers needed.

A great chorus of clicks sounds
and we remember
when giant Whooping Cranes
were among their number:
gone to extinction now.

We cherish these yearly travelers
who remind us we do well
to make homes for others,
set out food
for each beloved relative.

## Your Answer is Your Map

Birthright or chance, I wake each morning
in love with words, search their secrets,
wander their deserts,
summit their tallest peaks
with only the oxygen of my first breath.

*Qanuk, kaneq, muuaneq, nutaryuk, pirta:*
*snowflake, frost, needle-like, blizzard,*
*dusting, or soft deep snow.*
Inuit people have fifty names
for those crystals that fall from their sky.

Some languages have dozens of ways
to say *water* or *wind, friend* or *lover,*
two designations for father's
or mother's sister: shortcuts or excess
demanding we notice who we are?

I am a river dreaming of its tributaries,
exploring the abyss of each discovery.
The farther we stray from imagination,
the easier we forget. Loss of memory
leaves a permanent scar.

Creativity spars with fatigue on the tongue,
need courses through arteries,
meaning makes itself at home in flesh.
If you could choose, which would it be?
Your answer is your map.

# Change

There is nothing left but molecules of pain
seeping through the overgrown patios
of shattered homes, dark seawater as acid balm.

I wander among those who look or don't look
like me, their faces fade as I approach
and watch them turn their backs on invitation.

I want to scream our need to come together
and resist but when I open my mouth
only silence deadens the air I struggle to breathe.

I observe other mouths opening and closing
in a mockery of action, hear the rattle
of words colliding with hurricane winds.

We walk until we stumble. We shiver until
polar air freezes our skin and breaks us
before we can reach another willing hand.

An imagined chorus implores us to go home
but there is no home where we wander.
Oblivion seduces what energy we have left.

History will refer to us as Natives devoured
by colonization, Africans kidnapped
and forced to build nations on distant shores,

victims of every bully and every Holocaust
Latin America's Disappeared or those
who died beneath the rubble in Turkey and Syria.

One night we kissed our children goodnight,
dreamt a symphony or apple tree,
then morning brought the crushing vice of terror.

Escape was never meant to be part of the equation,
only a throat closing about one last gulp of air,
an image of rust corroding the hope of possibility.

But one brilliant molecule escapes that rampage
of disaster, an almost invisible seed
that will cultivate memory on this horizon

of defeat. Love's amnesia covers us with
buds of life springing up and out
through seasons of poisonous undergrowth.

Exuberant to be on the road again, we do not
stop to consider that fork ahead
where we may follow the leader one way

and risk tries to lure us another. Almost
wiped clean of memory
we do not know we must make a choice,

hold ourselves accountable. We may repeat
the cycle or use our power to bring
the change that will save us from ourselves.

*Uncollected Poems*

# Life as It Was

She closes her eyes and listens
to the wind while another
self-proclaimed Luddite
reads a book, not virtual but real
with its feel of paper
and faint scent of printer's ink
on every page.

These youngsters in Brooklyn
meet once a week
at Grand Army Plaza, a park
with trees, fresh air
and distant city sounds
reminding them the world
exists in real time.

They reject the social media vortex
pulling their generation
into a void where all is now,
instantaneous gratification
with no obligation to think
beyond an easy choice
of emoticons.

They say they are rediscovering
life as it was before a storm
with hundred-mile-an-hour winds
swept their minds clean
of imagination, touch,
and the privilege
of looking at one another.

## Moving from Escher to Silence

The dream keeps pulling you
off balance, making it hard
to draw one long breath
without counting in and out.
You wonder why you've been sent
to live in such cramped quarters,
a room not much larger
than three narrow beds,
yours farthest from the door.

No ancestors bring their
comforting secrets.
No one you know answers the phone.
Swarms of mosquitos fill the air
and you take the repellant
your host holds out,
trying to decide between
its poison
and a body bloody with bites.

It's one of those busy nights
that has you peering
from conflicting angles
into the unfamiliar room:
simultaneously on the narrow cot,

in your warm bed
and above it all, looking down,
conscious the dream
echoes repeat performance.

These are the nightmares that
disperse your waking hours
into complex patterns,
moving from Escher to silence,
morning to night.
When sleep takes you across
a dangerous border
you become an immigrant
of your imagination, a wanderer

whose papers will never be in order
and who dares cross over
without water to quench your thirst
or clothing warm enough
to brave the nor'easter
that batters your cheeks
wet with tears and chapped
from the raw shards of desert
your feet kick up.

The dream has its own obsessive rules
repeated in stormy crescendo
until you no longer know
if escaping that litany is possible.

Discordant sound deafens.
You may bring the puzzle pieces
with you when you wake
or retreat through night's portal in search
of an answer robust as memory.

# Failed Translation?

*On reading The Falling Sky: Words*
*of a Shaman* by Davi Kopenawa

*We call both mother and father mother,*
you say, *only begin to call*
*our father father*
*when we are older.* How much older?
You do not tell
and I try to imagine life's claim
upon your forest.

When you speak of that naming,
your words lodge themselves
between my teeth,
in the crooks of my elbows,
on the shadow
my body plants on earth
at high noon.

Your elders invented nicknames
that would accompany you
into adolescence. Gradually,
only gradually would you
acquire the one that follows you
through life: a word as vibrant
as animals and trees.

This morning I gazed at
a human fingerprint
photographed beside
a crosscut of tree rings,
two halves
of a living map:
our unique commonality.

You talk about the white invaders
who traveled up your river
imposing a name you didn't want,
its vibrations ugly to your ear
and misrepresenting your essence:
insult of sounds
sparring with expectation.

Because your words are not written,
you say, the path to them
is transparent, fixed inside.
You reach deep to retrieve them,
stretching a memory
that unfolds long as the river
that brings such threat.

You tell me my words are fragile,
must be written on image skins
or paper
so my people and I
won't forget them.

I listen to you in silence,
try to inhabit your premise.

I consider my own name—Margaret—
given at birth by a mother
who spoke it softly as she held me
to her breast. I have walked
with it 86 years now, written it
in Palmer script:
created its signature

by drawing it on what you call
paper skin.
I watch the name Margaret
charge through space, listen to it
on the lips of the woman I love,
hear it when a friend calls out to me,
smile as it signs my poems.

I write those three blood-red syllables
on this paper that holds my path,
pride of modernity.
You tell your story
at a distance I cannot cross
even as my beautiful language
registers both our scripts.

Is this about failed translation
or mouths shaped differently,

place and its time
giving us diverse landscapes
on which to grow,
disparate sounds
linking our histories?

# Waving Goodbye to the Shadow of Myself

Memories and the knowledge they bring
invade the great hall of my brain
as if in the baroque abundance
of a seventeenth century theater.
Those who know the performance by heart
crowd standing-room-only in the back
while the privileged rich
fan their bejeweled bodies
from elegant boxes closest to the stage.

In my altered image, muscles and tendons
stretch limber as in girlhood,
flawless skin and luxuriant hair
echo a time lost many years before.
My teeth line up, count themselves present
while ears try to trick me
into believing they can decipher
the broken murmur of streams
on a dying horizon.

Time's talent is in its tempo, slow motion
barely perceptible to the eye.
Hair's silver strands are only highlights
at first, and a wrinkle here or there
claim they can be repaired
with products advertised to restore

that ever-marketable youth.
Muscles promise return
through diligence of effort.

But my mirror takes a stand, refuses
to give back the youthful image,
shows instead a tired weathering,
seasons of living with and around
and over and through
all that came my way.
Rusty hinges push back folds
of mottled skin that thins with age,
my glory no longer a glittering crown.

I gave my fragile finger joints
to keys that spelled words,
my slender waist
to the children I birthed,
my hips to the hours
of sitting and thinking and writing,
feet to walking the circuitous trails
of battle in search of a justice
that would not come.

Bones splinter and break before
hitting bottom. Angry elbows
and knees want to shift position
but can't. Voice has lost its resonance

and crows like a high-pitched whistle
in the dark. Confidence stumbles
over itself, dragging blood and heat
behind in this awkward dance
that spars with death.

Still, memories continue to leap,
each glowing with dimming light.
Old energy struggles to keep today's
rhythm and breath line, the power
that will stretch this life I've pushed
against every known boundary,
planting the seeds for future women
who will look in their own mirrors
and wave goodbye to shadows of themselves.

## Silence

Silence is not the opposite of noise,
nor the absence of noise
but its own lexicon, a language
that invites you to listen carefully,
parse tempo, tone, bright lights and shadow,
and then translate it all
in the eye of the storm.

If you are not a dog, you may
miss the highest register.
If your memory is less than elephantine
you don't have a chance
of engaging history. Only blue whales
pursue their vowels and consonants
through the deepest water.

Don't be deterred by the shape of your ear,
how close your lips are to the desert
in pre-dawn cold, or where your eyes meet
the sounds of the universe
transcribed as abstract colors,
messages that live for centuries
without reaching their destination.

Silence is bigger and busier, it embraces
a code no Rosetta Stone can crack,
whispers even as it conveys its imaginary history
and deepest secrets.
If you can write and recite it at bedtime
to the one you love, the poem
will come to your rescue every time.

# Room 5007

1.

Eighty-six-year-old female, one kidney
and its half gone,
presents with dehydration,
fever, chills, weakness.
Arrived by ambulance.

When I tell the ambulance crew
they're doing a great job,
one laughs and says: It'll end
at the hospital door. Black humor:
familiar and comforting.

This emergency department
does what it can: 1 doctor
for 40 to 50 patients,
broken healthcare system
scrambling to keep up.

It's been corporate for a while
in this richest country
on earth, but I seek that glimmer
of humanity through obstacle course
of tubes, hum of confusion.

And the question rises about me
sucking all the air
from this small cubicle. Yet no one
is asking the question,
no power voice claims provenance.

2.

I've been admitted to a room
upstairs, but must wait
for one to become available.
Meaning someone else
must get well, or someone die.

I am the 86-year-old woman
carrying my history
in trembling hands, cared for
by hands from Cameroon,
India, Mexico.

The verdict is Sepsis
caused by E. Coli
shrieking through the rebel
highways and byways
of my blood.

Sudden images of the other: Africans,
their vacant eyes unfocussed
beyond the camera's range,

close a breach
no longer alien.

Differences fade as I barter
our shared humanity,
common sameness
of cause and effect,
intertwining of destinies.

3.

Floating from my own orbit
and back, I am conscious
there are billions of orbits,
each anchoring its own
solar spin.

We are not circling our
or any other sun
but black holes in a random cosmos
threatening to suck us
past oblivion.

What we have always known
taunts us now
from behind fingers laced
across expressionless eyes.
Not what they groomed us to expect.

A shift of meaning rethinks
all we've been taught
at schools that bled us dry
for what should be accessible to all:
discovery and choice.

We are reaping the sticky residue
of practices that weighed
excess and avarice, then chose
to bury their guilty heads
in shifting sands.

4.

In this hospital alone, those
of all ages and ills
reach to accept or fight
prognoses that will save
or end their lives.

I imagine the stories unfolding
behind those other doors:
The child whose chance at life
was much too brief, a grandmother
trying to say goodbye.

The charge nurse tells me the doctor
will get to me soon, he's just down
the hall. I think of him leaving one story

and entering another, disparate gambits
in this game of human chess.

Am I the devious Bishop or smart Knight,
the mighty King wearing his mask
of power or Queen
with her hidden agenda?
Am I just a Pawn in Conquest's path?

Worlds spin out of control
and collide. Humans
caught in corporate cruelty
must wage the contest
to its final piece.

5.

I know there is no master hand
manipulating this game
and I know it's not a game.
Histories of health and famine
signal one way, then another.

Infinite worlds spin on axes
anchoring hope
like scattered whisps of cloud.
Mine is so small it is lost
in the blinding array.

And then I am the only one
who exists, all others
fading like extinct languages
spoken by the last lips
able to shape their sounds.

Myself as random web of molecules
sparring with myself
as the brightest star in a firmament
of brilliant specks: a back and forth
that dizzies time and space.

For this is what I know for sure:
everything does not
happen for a reason, no matter
how hard I try to climb the mountain
or give myself to the valley.

6.

The question now: can my
body and will
do what must be done?
Can our generational victories
turn the cogs on this tired wheel?

From then on, it's one great dream
dreaming itself.

Doctors and nurses have only
bit parts in this drama
of formulae and lies.

Ancestors I never knew
dance about me.
Children and their children
take my hand. My woman
holds my eyes in hers.

The trick is to release without
letting go, let the gears
engage without worrying
about perfect fit or dissonance,
confident wholeness may come.

It will come, if it does, on wings
of hand-to-hand combat,
carrying the promise it will stay
only as long as the next crisis of confidence,
jubilant gasp of history.

7.

The machine that monitored
my heart, its moving lines
like waves
and blaring numbers
flickering red and green

was a 21st century Rosetta Stone
speaking crude poetry.
I remember a friend, one who
truly reads my poems,
saying she found an old one

called *Daughter of Lady Jaguar Shark*
and reread it
sitting on stairs in fading light.
She told me it said
all that needed to be said.

My tribute to the Mayan woman
who brightened her star
accompanying centuries of men
gives me the strength
to banish this invader from my body.

And I know those digital lines
and numbers on the screen
translate to the words
that run through my body,
fighting for survival.

8.

One day violent winds
bring hesitation,
each song something

I mimic perfectly
in resolute time.

The next, a new energy
pays a call and even
when its visits are brief,
premonition lifts me
on sturdy shoulders.

It could have gone either way
or some other way
still nameless in surprise,
painful or painless
in its gifts.

This time I made it through,
am still here
balanced between options
I could neither manage
nor control.

I might have left myself behind
but rallied instead
and kept moving,
asking questions without answers,
making tradeoffs with future.

9.

I have learned my body has wonders
up its sleeve, stories told
in languages I've never heard
and that will hold my hand
in times of need.

My orbit is no greater or smaller
than the next, my life
no more important than that
of the African nurse who takes
the time to smile at me.

What's more: our orbits depend
on one another, performance
larger than the sum of its parts.
I take my place in this scenario,
purpose in one hand, chance in the other.

The eighty-six-year-old woman goes home
to a changed world,
one built of straw and clay
rather than the zeros and ones
of our imposter knowledge.

Surviving or succumbing
is no longer the problem,

but how to use what time is left
to me, how I will bend its meaning
to past, future, now.

# About the Author

Margaret Randall (New York, 1936) is a poet, essayist, oral historian, translator, photographer, and social activist. She lived in Latin America for 23 years (in Mexico, Cuba, and Nicaragua). With Mexican poet Sergio Mondragón she founded, and from 1962 to 1969 co-edited, *El Corno Emplumado / The Plumed Horn*, a bilingual literary quarterly that published some of the best new work of the sixties. When she came home in 1984, the government ordered her deported because it found some of her writing to be "against the good order and happiness of the United States." With the support of The Center for Constitutional Rights as well as many writers and others, she won her case, and her citizenship was restored in 1989. Randall's most recent poetry titles include *Against Atrocity*, *Out of Violence into Poetry* (both from Wings Press), *Stormclouds Like Unkept Promises*, *Vertigo of Risk*, and *Home* (all from Casa Urraca Press). Among other recent titles are *Haydée Santamaría: She Led by Transgression* and *Che on My Mind* (a feminist poet's reminiscence of Che Guevara (both from Duke University Press), *Thinking about Thinking* (essays, from Casa Urraca), and *My Life in 100 Objects*, *Artists in My Life*, and *Luck* (all from New Village Press). *Your Answer is Your Map* is a "bus-ticket" or broadside published by Bob & Susan Arnold's Longhouse in Summer 2023. In 2020 Duke published her memoir, *I Never Left Home: Poet, Feminist, Revolutionary*. Two of Randall's photographs are in the Capitol Art Collection in Santa Fe. She has also devoted herself to translation, producing *The Oval Portrait, Contemporary Cuban Women Writers and Artists* by Soleida Ríos, *When Rains Become Floods* by Lurgio Galván Sánchez, *You Can Cross the Massacre on Foot* by Freddy Prestol Castillo, *The Art of Memory: An Ethnographer's Journey* by Stefano Varese, *Dictated by Fire / Lo que el fuego dictó* by Juan Antonio Hernández, and *Only the Road / Solo el camino*, *an anthology of eight decades of Cuban poetry*, among many other titles. Randall received the 2017 *Medalla al Mérito Literario* from *Literatura en el Bravo*, Ciudad Juárez, Mexico. In 2018 she was awarded the "Poet of two Hemispheres" prize by *Poesía en Paralelo Cero* in Quito, Ecuador. Cuba's Casa de las Américas awarded her its prestigious Haydée Santamaría medal in 2019. In 2019 she was awarded an honorary doctorate of letters from the University of New Mexico and in 2022 she received the City of Albuquerque's Creative Bravo Award. Randall lives in Albuquerque with her wife of more than 36 years, the painter Barbara Byers, and travels extensively to read, lecture and teach.

# About the Authors of the Introduction

Katherine M. Hedeen's latest book-length translations include *night badly written* (Action Books) and *tasks* (coimpress, longlisted for the Best Translated Book Award, shortlisted for the National Translation Award, 2017) by Víctor Rodríguez Núñez, and *Nothing Out of This World* (Smokestack), an anthology of contemporary Cuban poetry which won the English PEN Award. She is the Poetry Translation Editor for the *Kenyon Review* and the recipient of two NEA Translation Project Grants. She is a Professor of Spanish at Kenyon College.

Víctor Rodríguez Núñez (Havana, 1955) is a poet, journalist, literary critic, translator, and scholar. He has published fifty books of poetry throughout the Americas, Europe, and Asia, and his work has received many major awards in the Spanish-speaking world, most recently, Spain's coveted Loewe Poetry Prize. He has compiled three anthologies that define his poetic generation, as well as another of 20th century Cuban poetry, *La poesía del siglo XX en Cuba* (2011). He has brought out various critical editions, introductions, and essays on Spanish American poets. One of Cuba's most outstanding contemporary writers, he divides his time between Gambier, Ohio, where he is Professor of Spanish at Kenyon College, and Havana.

**W**ings **Press** was founded in 1975 by Joanie Whitebird and Joseph F. Lomax, both deceased, as "an informal association of artists and cultural mythologists dedicated to the preservation of the literature of the nation of Texas." Publisher, editor and designer from 1995 until the final Wings volume appeared in 2023, Bryce Milligan was honored to carry on and expand that mission to include the finest in American writing—meaning all of the Americas, without commercial considerations clouding the decision to publish or not to publish.

Wings Press produced over 200 multi-cultural books, chapbooks, ebooks, recordings and broadsides intended to enlighten the human spirit and enliven the mind. The publisher long believed that writing is a transformational art form capable of changing the world, primarily by allowing us to glimpse something of each other's souls. Good writing is innovative, insightful, and interesting, but most of all it is honest. As Bob Dylan put it, "To live outside the law, you must be honest."

Wings Press was committed to treating the planet itself as a partner. Thus the press used as much recycled material as possible, from the paper on which the books were/are printed to the boxes in which they were/are shipped.

As Robert Dana wrote in *Against the Grain*, "Small press publishing is personal publishing. In essence, it's a matter of personal vision, personal taste and courage, and personal friendships." Welcome to our world.

## Colophon

This first edition of *Time's Language II: Selected Poems 2019-2023*, by Margaret Randall, has been printed on 60 pound "natural" paper containing a percentage of recycled fiber. Titles have been set in Nueva Standard type, the text in Adobe Caslon type. This book was designed by Bryce Milligan.

Wings Press titles are distributed to the trade by the Independent Publishers Group
www.ipgbook.com
and in Europe by Gazelle
www.gazellebookservices.co.uk

*Also available as an ebook.*